the **low** carb cookbook

low carb not no carb

the **low** carb cookbook

low carb not no carb

MURDOCH
B O O K S

Published by Murdoch Books®, Pier 8/9, 23 Hickson Road, Millers Point, NSW 2000, AUSTRALIA
Murdoch Books UK Ltd, Erico House, 6th Floor North, 93-99 Upper Richmond Road,
Putney, London SW15 2TG.

Editor: Anouska Jones **Design:** Kerry Klinner; SASO Content and Design
Production Controller: Monika Paratore

National Library of Australia Cataloguing-in-Publication Data.
Low carb cookbook. Includes index. ISBN 1740 453 859.
1. Low-carbohydrate diet - Recipes.
641.56383

Printed by Midas Printing (Asia) Ltd. PRINTED IN CHINA.

USEFUL INFORMATION

The recipes in this book were developed using a tablespoon measure of 20 ml. In some other countries the tablespoon is 15 ml. For most recipes this difference will not be noticeable but, for recipes using baking powder, gelatine, bicarbonate of soda, small amounts of flour and cornflour, we suggest that, if you are using the smaller tablespoon, you add an extra teaspoon for each tablespoon.

The recipes in this book are written using convenient cup measurements. You can buy special measuring cups in the supermarket or use an ordinary household cup: first you need to check it holds 250 ml (8 fl oz) by filling it with water and measuring the water (pour it into a measuring jug or a carton that you know holds 250 ml). This cup can then be used for both liquid and dry cup measurements.

Liquid cup measures

1/4 cup	60 ml	2 fluid oz
1/3 cup	80 ml	2 3/4 fluid oz
1/2 cup	125 ml	4 fluid oz
3/4 cup	180 ml	6 fluid oz
1 cup	250 ml	8 fluid oz

Spoon measures

1/4 teaspoon	1.25 ml
1/2 teaspoon	2.5 ml
1 teaspoon	5 ml
1 tablespoon	20 ml

Nutritional Information

The nutritional information given for each recipe does not include any garnishes or accompaniments, such as rice or pasta, unless they are included in specific quantities in the ingredients list. The nutritional values are approximations and can be affected by biological and seasonal variations in foods, the unknown composition of some manufactured foods and uncertainty in the dietary database. Nutrient data given are derived primarily from the NUTTAB95 database produced by the Australian and New Zealand Food Authority.

Oven Temperatures
You may find cooking times vary depending on the oven you are using. For fan-forced ovens, as a general rule, set oven temperature to 20°C lower than indicated in the recipe.

Note: Those who might be at risk from the effects of salmonella food poisoning (the elderly, pregnant women, young children and those suffering from immune deficiency diseases) should consult their GP with any concerns about eating raw eggs.

Alternative names (UK/US)

bicarbonate of soda	—	baking soda
besan flour	—	chickpea flour
capsicum	—	red or green bell pepper
chickpeas	—	garbanzo beans
cornflour	—	cornstarch
fresh coriander	—	cilantro
single cream	—	cream
aubergine	—	eggplant
flat-leaf parsley	—	Italian parsley
hazelnut	—	filbert
minced beef	—	ground beef
plain flour	—	all-purpose flour
polenta	—	cornmeal
prawn	—	shrimp
Roma tomato	—	plum or egg tomato
sambal oelek	—	chilli paste
mangetout	—	snow pea
spring onion	—	scallion
thick cream	—	heavy cream
tomato purée	—	tomato paste
courgette	—	zucchini

Weight

10 g	1/4 oz	220 g	7 oz	425 g	14 oz
30 g	1 oz	250 g	8 oz	475 g	15 oz
60 g	2 oz	275 g	9 oz	500 g	1 lb
90 g	3 oz	300 g	10 oz	600 g	1 1/4 lb
125 g	4 oz	330 g	11 oz	650 g	1 lb 5 oz
150 g	5 oz	375 g	12 oz	750 g	1 1/2 lb
185 g	6 oz	400 g	13 oz	1 kg	2 lb

Contents

Introduction

If you're one of those people who has religiously chosen high carbohydrate/low fat foods for years in an effort to keep your weight down, the thought of switching to a diet that is high in protein and fats probably makes you feel very uncomfortable indeed.

Rest assured there is method in the apparent madness, and many people feel and look great on a low carb diet.

As with all weight-loss programs, it's important to have a medical check-up before you start. If you are pregnant, breast-feeding, epileptic or have kidney disease, a low carbohydrate diet is not for you. If you are taking medically prescribed diuretics, you should consult your doctor before you start, and if you are diabetic you should only consider such a program under the professional care of your dietician or doctor.

So how does it work?

When you say 'I need to lose weight', what you really mean is: 'I need to reduce my stored body fat' — and the way to do this is to use the stored fat as an energy source to power your body's metabolic processes.

Most of the time, your body derives its energy from recently consumed carbohydrates, which it uses as a source of cellular energy after converting them to glucose. The glucose moves from your digestive system into the blood (hence the term 'blood sugar'), triggering the secretion of the hormone insulin, which ensures that the blood sugar is transported into your cells where it is available to use as a source of cellular energy.

A diet high in carbohydrates may actually cause you to gain weight, since any excess glucose is stored for later use, either as glycogen (in the muscles and liver) or as body fat. This is particularly likely to occur if you choose foods that are high in refined (or processed) carbohydrates, such as sugar and wheat flour.

Consistently eating a high carbohydrate diet may also trigger a vicious circle in which insulin is over-produced, resulting in fluctuating blood sugar levels, which in turn cause energy levels to plummet, setting up cravings for yet more carbohydrates. Over a prolonged period, this repetitive sequence of events leads to the consumption of ever-increasing quantities of carbohydrates, and also makes the cells less and less sensitive to the effects of insulin (a situation referred to as insulin resistance). People in this situation commonly feel sluggish, tired, irritable, overweight, and generally unhealthy.

Insulin resistance and excessive consumption of the wrong type of carbohydrates are fast emerging as some of the major culprits behind spiralling levels of obesity, and are also considered to be risk factors for the development of diabetes and cardiovascular disease.

The reason that following a low carbohydrate diet works for so many people is that it helps to control the body's production and utilization of insulin and allows stored fat to be used as the body's energy source, rather than recently consumed carbohydrates.

After two to three days on a low carbohydrate diet, the body shifts from using carbohydrates as its energy source, and starts to burn stored fat instead (the medical term is 'lipolysis' — literally, 'fat breakdown'). When this happens, your body gives off chemical compounds called ketones, and you may notice changes to the smell of your urine or breath. This is a sign that you have shifted into fat-burning mode, and is nothing to be alarmed about. (There's a medical term for this too — 'ketosis', the production of ketones).

In order for lipolysis to occur, most people need to markedly reduce their carbohydrate intake and focus instead on eating relatively large amounts of oils (or 'fats') and protein (such as eggs, red meat, poultry and seafood), neither of which involve insulin in their absorption and utilization.

It is important to be aware that although many people report increased energy levels and improved clarity of thought once lipolysis commences, it is also quite common to experience transient feelings of sluggishness and fatigue. If this continues beyond a few days, add a few extra grams of carbohydrate to your diet. Seek the assistance of your health professional before continuing with a low carb diet if the symptoms are still present a few days later.

Key points

Not all carbohydrates are the same. Above all, avoid refined carbs, which rapidly convert into glucose in your body. Foods high in refined carbohydrates include sugar, flour (in bread, cakes, breakfast cereals etc), and white rice.

For the purposes of weight loss, it is also useful to think of starchy vegetables such as potatoes as a form of refined carbohydrate, as starches are also quickly converted to glucose.

As a general rule, if you don't add sugar or flour to any foods you prepare yourself, and don't eat any processed or packaged food at all, you will go a long way towards skipping refined carbohydrates. Limit carbohydrate intake to around 20 g per day, which should predominantly be eaten in the form of vegetables such as spinach, lettuce, broccoli and other salad greens. When taken as veggies like these, 20 g of carbohydrate equates to either three cups of uncooked salad vegetables, or two cups of salad vegetables plus $2/3$ cup cooked low carbohydrate vegetables.

Note that although it is a form of carbohydrate, fibre is indigestible (or 'unavailable'), and so does not contribute to blood sugar elevation and insulin secretion — nor does it need to be included when calculating a food's carbohydrate content.

Learn to read the nutritional panel on food labels. To work out how many grams of carbohydrate a food will contribute to your daily allowance, simply subtract the fibre content from the total carbohydrate content listed on the label.

In order to maintain regularity and avoid constipation, fibre content should be an important daily consideration when choosing your allowance of carbohydrate foods. If you experience constipation, add a fibre source such as psyllium husks or 100% wheat bran to your diet in small quantities — but don't forget to choose a product that's sugar-free.

Drink at least two litres of water each day to help avoid constipation, and to ensure that you are efficiently eliminating body wastes in your urine.

To be on the safe side and ensure that you're not missing out on essential vitamins and minerals, take a good multi-vitamin and mineral supplement whilst you are following the low carb diet. Be sure to choose one with reasonable doses (e.g. 25-50 mg of each of the B vitamins and around 250 mg vitamin C) and from a reputable company. This is particularly important as you will be eating minimal amounts of fruit on this eating plan.

The recipes in this book have been created in our special test kitchens, where recipes are double-tested by a team of home economists and nutritionists to achieve a high standard of success every time.

The nutritional values shown relate to an average-sized portion of the recipe. The nutritional values of other accompaniments shown (such as rice, bread, salad and potatoes) which may have been used for styling purposes, are NOT included in the nutritional analysis.

The average carbohydrate content, per portion, of some common foods:

Brown rice	58 g	White rice	56 g
Bagel	46 g	Baguette	22 g
Baked potato	22 g	Chips	59 g
Broad beans	7 g		

Healthy low carb eating

Eat liberally	Proteins	Meat (e.g. lamb, beef, pork, veal)
		Eggs and poultry (e.g. chicken, turkey, duck)
		Fish (e.g. salmon, tuna, trout, mackerel, sardines)
		Shellfish (e.g. prawns, lobster, crayfish, mussels)
	Fats	Salad oils (e.g. olive oil, avocado oil, walnut oil)
		Cooking oils (e.g. safflower oil, canola oil)
		Avocado, macadamia nuts
	Salad vegetables	Green leafy vegetables including: chicory, endive, lettuce (cos, iceberg, romaine etc), parsley, rocket, sorrel, spinach
		Other water-rich salad vegetables including: alfalfa, asparagus, bamboo shoots, broccoli, cabbage, capsicum, cauliflower, celery, chives, cucumbers, eggplants, fennel, green beans, leeks, mushrooms, okra, onions, radishes, spring onions, snow peas, tomatoes, water chestnut, zucchinis
Eat moderately	Cheese (contains lactose, a carbohydrate)	Cheddar, goats' cheese, Gouda, mozzarella, Swiss (avoid fresh cheeses, such as cottage cheese, which contain more carbohydrates)
Avoid	Refined carbohydrates	Sugar, honey, alcohol, glucose (including carbonated beverages), processed wheat and flour products (e.g. bread, cakes, biscuits, breakfast cereal)
	Starchy vegetables	Potato, sweet potato, yam, parsnip, carrot, beetroot
	Grains	Rice, rice cakes
		Oats and porridge
		Barley, rye, millet
	Legumes & pulses	Beans, peas, lentils
	Fruit	Fresh fruit including: apples, bananas, cherries, figs, grapes, lemons, melons, mangoes, oranges, paw paw, pineapple, raspberries, watermelon
		Dried fruit including: apples, apricots, pears, sultanas, raisins, dried figs
		Fruit juice

Recipes

5 g and under

Baked Ricotta with Preserved Lemon and Semi-dried Tomatoes

2 kg (4 lb) round ricotta cheese
olive oil
2 cloves garlic, crushed
1 preserved lemon, rinsed, pith and flesh
removed, cut into thin strips
150 g (5 oz) semi-dried tomatoes, roughly
chopped
1 cup (30 g/1 oz) finely chopped fresh flat-leaf
parsley

1 cup (50 g/1¾ oz) chopped fresh coriander
leaves
⅓ cup (80 ml/2¾ fl oz) extra virgin olive oil
3 tablespoons lemon juice

PREPARATION TIME 15 minutes + 10 minutes
standing
TOTAL COOKING TIME 30 minutes
SERVES 8–10

1 Preheat the oven to very hot 250°C (500°F/Gas 10). Place the ricotta on a baking tray lined with baking paper, brush lightly with the olive oil and bake for 20–30 minutes, or until golden brown. Leave for 10 minutes then, using egg flips, transfer to a large platter. (If possible, have someone help you move the ricotta.)

2 Meanwhile, place the garlic, preserved lemon, semi-dried tomato, parsley, coriander, oil and lemon juice in a bowl and mix together well.

3 Spoon the dressing over the baked ricotta and serve with crusty bread. It is delicious hot or cold.

NUTRITION PER SERVE Protein 20 g; Fat 30 g; **Carbohydrate 3 g**; Dietary Fibre 0.5 g; Cholesterol 95 mg; 1542 kJ (368 cal)
NOTE Bread shown as a serving suggestion. Carbohydrate content not included in nutrition per serve.

Tomato and Basil Salad

6 ripe Roma tomatoes
1 sliced red onion

Dressing
1 crushed garlic clove
2 tablespoons balsamic vinegar
1 cup (60 g/2 oz) shredded basil leaves

PREPARATION TIME 5 minutes
SERVES 4

1 Quarter Roma tomatoes and mix with the red
onion, garlic clove, balsamic vinegar and shredded
basil leaves. Toss, season and set aside for
10 minutes, then transfer to a shallow dish. (If
you find raw onion too strong, put it in a bowl
and cover with boiling water for 5 minutes.
Drain well.)

NUTRITION PER SERVE Protein 2 g; Fat 0 g; **Carbohydrate 5 g**; Dietary Fibre 2 g; Cholesterol 0 mg; 120 kJ (30 cal)

Stuffed Mushroom Salad

20 button mushrooms
$\frac{1}{4}$ cup (60 g/2 oz) pesto, chilled
100 g (3$\frac{1}{2}$ oz) rocket leaves
1 green oakleaf lettuce
12 small black olives
$\frac{1}{3}$ cup (50 g/1$\frac{3}{4}$ oz) sliced semi-dried or
sun-dried tomatoes
1 tablespoon roughly chopped basil
Parmesan shavings, to serve

Dressing
$\frac{1}{3}$ cup (80 ml/2$\frac{3}{4}$ fl oz) olive oil
1 tablespoon white wine vinegar
1 teaspoon Dijon mustard

PREPARATION TIME 25 minutes
SERVES 4

1 Trim the mushroom stalks level with the caps and scoop out the remaining stalk with a melon baller. Spoon the pesto into the mushrooms.

2 To make the dressing, whisk together all the ingredients. Season with salt and pepper, to taste.

3 Arrange the rocket and lettuce leaves on a serving plate and top with the mushrooms, olives, tomato and basil. Drizzle the dressing over the salad and top with the Parmesan shavings. Serve immediately.

Hint
Home-made pesto is preferable for this recipe.
To make your own, process 1 cup (30 g/1 oz) loosely packed basil leaves, 2 tablespoons pine nuts and $\frac{1}{4}$ cup (25 g/$\frac{3}{4}$ oz) grated Parmesan in a food processor to form a smooth paste. Gradually pour in $\frac{1}{4}$ cup (60 ml/2 fl oz) olive oil in a steady stream with the motor running. Process until combined.

NUTRITION PER SERVE Protein 9 g; Fat 35 g; **Carbohydrate 2 g**; Dietary Fibre 3 g; Cholesterol 15 mg; 1525 kJ (365 cal)

Tofu Salad with Ginger Miso Dressing

90 ml (3 fl oz) light soy sauce
2 teaspoons soy bean oil
2 cloves garlic, crushed
1 teaspoon grated fresh ginger
1 teaspoon chilli paste
500 g (1 lb) firm tofu, cut into small cubes
400 g (13 oz) mesclun leaves
1 Lebanese cucumber, finely sliced
250 g (8 oz) cherry tomatoes, halved
2 teaspoons soy bean oil, extra

Dressing
2 teaspoons white miso paste (see NOTE)
2 tablespoons mirin
1 teaspoon sesame oil
1 teaspoon grated fresh ginger
1 teaspoon finely chopped chives
1 tablespoon toasted sesame seeds

PREPARATION TIME 20 minutes + overnight marinating
TOTAL COOKING TIME 5 minutes
SERVES 4

1 Mix together the tamari, soy bean oil, garlic, ginger, chilli paste and ½ teaspoon salt in a bowl. Add the tofu and mix until well coated. Marinate for at least 10 minutes, or preferably overnight. Drain and reserve the marinade.

2 To make the dressing, combine the miso with ½ cup (125 ml/4 fl oz) hot water and leave until the miso dissolves. Add the mirin, sesame oil, ginger, chives and sesame seeds, and stir until beginning to thicken.

3 Put the mesclun leaves, cucumber and tomato in a serving bowl.

4 Heat the extra soy bean oil on a chargrill or hotplate. Add the tofu and cook over medium heat for 4 minutes, or until golden brown. Pour on the reserved marinade and cook for a further 1 minute over high heat. Remove from the grill and cool for 5 minutes.

5 Add the tofu to the salad, drizzle with the dressing and toss well.

Note
Miso is Japanese bean paste and is commonly used in soups, dressings, on grilled foods and as a flavouring for pickles.

NUTRITION PER SERVE Protein 12 g; Fat 8 g; **Carbohydrate 4 g**; Dietary Fibre 4 g; Cholesterol 0 mg; 590 kJ (140 cal)

Japanese Scallop and Ginger Salad

300 g (10 oz) fresh scallops, without roe
2 cups (100 g/3 oz) baby English spinach leaves
1 small red capsicum, cut into very fine strips
50 g (1 ½ oz) bean sprouts
30 ml (1 fl oz) sake
1 tablespoon lime juice

2 teaspoons shaved palm sugar
1 teaspoon fish sauce

PREPARATION TIME 10 minutes
TOTAL COOKING TIME 5 minutes
SERVES 4

1 Remove any veins, membrane or hard white muscle from the scallops. Lightly brush a chargrill plate with oil. Cook the scallops in batches on the chargrill plate for 1 minute each side, or until cooked.

2 Divide the English spinach leaves, capsicum and bean sprouts among four serving plates. Arrange the scallops over the top.

3 To make the dressing, whisk together the sake, lime juice, palm sugar and fish sauce. Pour over the salad and serve immediately.

Note
Sprinkle with toasted sesame seeds as a garnish.

NUTRITION PER SERVE Protein 10 g; Fat 0.5 g; **Carbohydrate 3.5 g**; Dietary Fibre 1.5 g; Cholesterol 25 mg; 274 kJ (65 cal)

Chargrilled Vegetable Terrine

350 g (11 oz) ricotta
2 cloves garlic, crushed
8 large slices chargrilled eggplant, drained
(see NOTE)
10 slices chargrilled red capsicum, drained
8 slices chargrilled zucchini, drained
45 g (1 1/2 oz) rocket leaves
3 marinated artichokes, drained and sliced

85 g (3 oz) semi-dried tomatoes, drained and chopped
100 g (3 1/2 oz) marinated mushrooms, drained and halved

PREPARATION TIME 30 minutes + overnight refrigeration
SERVES 8

1 Line a 24 x 13 x 6 cm (9 x 5 x 2½ inch) loaf tin with plastic wrap, leaving a generous amount hanging over the sides. Place the ricotta and garlic in a bowl and beat until smooth. Season with salt and pepper to taste and set aside.

2 Line the base of the tin with half the eggplant, cutting and fitting to cover the base. Top with a layer of half the capsicum, then all the zucchini slices. Spread evenly with the ricotta mixture and press down firmly. Place the rocket leaves on top of the ricotta. Arrange the artichoke, tomato and mushrooms in three rows lengthways on top of the ricotta.

3 Top with another layer of capsicum and finish with the eggplant. Fold the overhanging plastic wrap over the top of the terrine. Put a piece of cardboard on top and weigh it down with weights or small food cans. Refrigerate the terrine overnight.

4 To serve, peel back the plastic wrap and turn the terrine out onto a plate. Remove the plastic wrap and cut into thick slices.

Note
You can buy chargrilled eggplant, capsicum and zucchini, and marinated mushrooms and artichokes at delicatessens.

Storage
Cover any leftovers with plastic wrap and store in the refrigerator for up to 2 days.

NUTRITION PER SERVE Protein 6 g; Fat 5 g; **Carbohydrate 3 g**; Dietary Fibre 2 g; Cholesterol 20 mg; 350 kJ (85 cal)

Spinach and Feta Frittatas

150 g (5 oz) English spinach leaves
1 garlic clove, crushed
2 eggs
2 egg whites
¼ cup (60 ml/2 fl oz) skim milk
2 tablespoons grated Parmesan

70 g (2½ oz) low-fat feta, cut into 1 cm (½ in) cubes (you should have 18 cubes)

PREPARATION TIME 15 minutes
COOKING TIME 20 minutes
MAKES 6

1 Preheat the oven to moderately hot 200°C (400°F/Gas 6). Place the washed spinach leaves and garlic in a saucepan, cover and steam for 3–5 minutes, or until the spinach is wilted.

2 Cool the spinach slightly and squeeze any excess liquid out of the leaves, then roughly chop. Place the eggs, egg whites, skim milk and Parmesan in a bowl, and whisk to combine. Stir in the spinach. Season with salt and ground black pepper.

3 Spoon the spinach mixture into six ½ cup (125 ml/4 fl oz) non-stick muffin holes, filling each three-quarters full. Place three cubes of low-fat feta on top and press lightly into the mixture. Bake for 15 minutes, or until the frittatas are golden and set. Serve immediately.

Note
The mixture has a soufflé effect and will deflate quite quickly.

NUTRITION PER FRITTATA Protein 8 g; Fat 5 g; **Carbohydrate 0 g**; Dietary Fibre 0.5 g; Cholesterol 100 mg; 336 kJ (80 Cal)

Steamed Prawn Nori Rolls

500 g (1 lb) peeled raw prawns, deveined
1 ½ tablespoons fish sauce
1 tablespoon sake
2 tablespoons chopped fresh coriander
1 large fresh kaffir lime leaf,
finely shredded
1 tablespoon lime juice
2 teaspoons sweet chilli sauce
1 egg white, lightly beaten
5 sheets nori

Dipping sauce
¼ cup (60 ml/2 fl oz) sake
¼ cup (60 ml/2 fl oz) soy sauce
1 tablespoon mirin
1 tablespoon lime juice

PREPARATION TIME 15 minutes + 1 hour
refrigeration
TOTAL COOKING TIME 5 minutes
MAKES 25

1 Process the prawns in a food processor or blender
with the fish sauce, sake, coriander, kaffir lime
leaf, lime juice and sweet chilli sauce until smooth.
Add the egg white and mix for a few seconds to
just combine.

2 Lay the nori sheets on a flat surface and spread
some prawn mixture over each sheet, leaving a
clear border at one end. Roll up tightly, cover and
refrigerate for 1 hour to firm. Using a very sharp
knife, trim the ends, then cut into slices.

3 Place the rolls in a lined bamboo steamer, cover
and steam over a wok of simmering water, making
sure it doesn't touch the water. Steam for
5 minutes, or until heated through.

4 For the dipping sauce, thoroughly mix all the
ingredients together in a small bowl. Serve with
the nori rolls.

NUTRITION PER ROLL Protein 4 g; Fat 0.5 g; **Carbohydrate 0.5 g**; Dietary Fibre 0.5 g; Cholesterol 39.5 mg; 95 kJ (23 cal)

Combination Dim Sims

6 dried Chinese mushrooms
200 g (6½ oz) lean pork mince
30 g (1 oz) pork fat, finely chopped
100 g (3⅓ oz) raw prawn meat, finely chopped
2 spring onions, finely chopped
1 tablespoon sliced bamboo shoots, finely chopped
1 celery stick, finely chopped

3 teaspoons cornflour
2 teaspoons soy sauce
1 teaspoon caster sugar
30 won ton or egg noodle wrappers

PREPARATION TIME 1 hour + 1 hour refrigeration
TOTAL COOKING TIME 30 minutes
MAKES about 30

1 Soak the mushrooms in 1 cup (250 ml/8 fl oz) hot water for 10 minutes, drain and chop the caps finely, discarding the hard stalks.

2 Mix together the mushrooms, pork mince, pork fat, prawn, spring onion, bamboo shoots and celery. Mix the cornflour, soy, sugar and salt and pepper into a smooth paste and then stir into the pork mixture. Cover and refrigerate for 1 hour.

3 Work with one wrapper at a time, keeping the rest covered with a damp tea towel to prevent drying out. Place 1 tablespoon of filling in the centre of each wrapper. Moisten the edges with water and fold the corners into the centre. Press the corners together to seal. Place on a lightly floured surface.

4 Line the base of a bamboo steamer with a circle of baking paper. Arrange the dim sims on the paper in batches, cover and cook over a pan of simmering water for 8 minutes, or until the wrappers are firm and the filling is cooked. Serve with chilli or soy sauce.

NUTRITION PER DIM SIM Protein 3 g; Fat 2 g; **Carbohydrate 1 g**; Dietary Fibre 0 g; Cholesterol 10 mg; 77 kJ (18 cal)

Roasted Red Capsicum Soup

4 large red capsicums
4 ripe tomatoes
2 tablespoons oil
1 red onion, chopped
1 clove garlic, crushed
4 cups (1 litre/32 fl oz) vegetable stock

1 teaspoon sweet chilli sauce
Parmesan and pesto, to garnish

PREPARATION TIME 50 minutes
TOTAL COOKING TIME 1 hour
SERVES 6

1 Cut the capsicums into large flat pieces, removing the seeds and membrane. Place skin-side-up under a hot grill until blackened. Leave covered with a tea towel until cool, then peel away the skin and chop the flesh.

2 Score a small cross in the base of each tomato, put them in a large heatproof bowl and cover with boiling water. Leave for 1 minute, then plunge into cold water and peel the skin from the cross. Cut in half, scoop out the seeds and roughly chop the flesh.

3 Heat the oil in a large heavy-based pan and add the onion. Cook over medium heat for 10 minutes, stirring frequently, until very soft. Add the garlic and cook for a further minute. Add the capsicum, tomato and stock; bring to the boil, reduce the heat and simmer for about 20 minutes.

4 Purée the soup in a food processor or blender until smooth (in batches if necessary). Return to the pan to reheat gently and stir in the chilli sauce. Serve topped with shavings of Parmesan and a little pesto.

NUTRITION PER SERVE Protein 3 g; Fat 7 g; **Carbohydrate 5 g**; Dietary Fibre 2 g; Cholesterol 0 mg; 380 kJ (90 cal)

Cream of Asparagus Soup

1 kg (2 lb) asparagus spears
30 g (1 oz) butter
1 onion, finely chopped
1 litre (32 fl oz) vegetable stock
¼ cup (7 g/¼ oz) basil leaves, chopped
1 teaspoon celery salt
1 cup (250 ml/8 fl oz) cream

PREPARATION TIME 20 minutes
TOTAL COOKING TIME 55 minutes
SERVES 4–6

1 Break off the woody ends from the asparagus (hold both ends of the spear and bend it gently—the woody end will snap off and can be thrown away) and trim off the tips. Blanch the tips in boiling water for 1–2 minutes, refresh in cold water and set aside. Chop the asparagus stems into large pieces.

2 Melt the butter in a large pan and cook the onion for 3–4 minutes over medium-low heat, or until soft and golden. Add the chopped asparagus stems and cook for 1–2 minutes, stirring continuously.

3 Add the stock, basil and celery salt. Bring to the boil, reduce the heat and simmer, covered, for 30 minutes.

4 Check that the asparagus is well cooked and soft. If not, simmer for a further 10 minutes. Set aside and allow to cool slightly.

5 Pour into a processor and process in batches until smooth. Then sieve into a clean pan. Return to the heat, pour in the cream and gently reheat. Do not allow the soup to boil. Season to taste with salt and white pepper. Add the asparagus tips and serve immediately.

Hint
If you are not using home-made stock, always taste before adding seasoning to your soup—shop-bought stock can be very salty.

NUTRITION PER SERVE Protein 6 g; Fat 22 g; **Carbohydrate 5 g**; Dietary Fibre 3 g; Cholesterol 70 mg; 990 kJ (237 cal)

Tom Yam Goong

500 g (1 lb) raw prawns
1 tablespoon oil
2 tablespoons Thai red curry paste
2 tablespoons tamarind purée
2 teaspoons turmeric
1 teaspoon chopped red chillies
4 kaffir lime leaves, shredded
2 tablespoons fish sauce

2 tablespoons lime juice
2 teaspoons soft brown sugar
fresh coriander leaves, to garnish

PREPARATION TIME 25 minutes
TOTAL COOKING TIME 45 minutes
SERVES 4–6

1 Peel and devein the prawns, leaving the tails intact. Heat the oil in a large pan and cook the prawn shells and heads for 10 minutes over medium-high heat, tossing frequently, until the heads are deep orange.

2 Add 1 cup (250 ml/8 fl oz) water and the curry paste. Boil for 5 minutes, or until reduced slightly. Add 2 litres water and simmer for 20 minutes. Strain, discarding the shells and heads, and return the stock to the pan.

3 Add the tamarind, turmeric, chilli and lime leaves, bring to the boil and cook for 2 minutes. Add the prawns and cook for 5 minutes, or until pink. Add the fish sauce, lime juice and sugar. Garnish with coriander leaves.

Hint
If you can't find tamarind purée, soak one quarter of a block of tamarind in warm water for 10 minutes, work the mixture with your fingertips and remove the stones.

NUTRITION PER SERVE Protein 17 g; Fat 6 g; **Carbohydrate 2 g**; Dietary Fibre 0 g; Cholesterol 125 mg; 560 kJ (135 cal)

Tofu in Black Bean Sauce

⅓ cup (80 ml/2¾ fl oz) vegetable stock
2 teaspoons cornflour
2 teaspoons Chinese rice wine (see NOTE)
1 teaspoon sesame oil
1 tablespoon soy sauce
2 tablespoons peanut oil
450 g (14 oz) firm tofu, diced
2 cloves garlic, very finely chopped
2 teaspoons finely chopped fresh ginger

3 tablespoons fermented black beans, rinsed and very finely chopped
4 spring onions, cut on the diagonal
1 red capsicum, cut into cubes
300 g (10 oz) baby bok choy, chopped

PREPARATION TIME 20 minutes
TOTAL COOKING TIME 15 minutes
SERVES 4

1 Combine the vegetable stock, cornflour, rice wine, sesame oil, soy sauce, ½ teaspoon salt and freshly ground black pepper in a small bowl.

2 Heat a wok over medium heat, add the peanut oil and swirl to coat. Add the tofu and stir-fry in two batches for 3 minutes each batch, or until lightly browned. Remove with a slotted spoon and drain on paper towels. Discard any bits of tofu stuck to the wok or floating in the oil.

3 Add the garlic and ginger and stir-fry for 30 seconds. Toss in the black beans and spring onion and stir-fry for 30 seconds. Add the capsicum and stir-fry for 1 minute. Add the bok choy and stir-fry for a further 2 minutes. Return the tofu to the wok and stir gently. Pour in the sauce and stir gently for 2–3 minutes, or until the sauce has thickened slightly. Serve immediately.

Note
Chinese rice wine is an alcoholic liquid made from cooked glutinous rice and millet mash which has been fermented with yeast, then aged for a period of 10 to 100 years. With a sherry-like taste, it is used as both a drink and a cooking liquid.

NUTRITION PER SERVE Protein 13 g; Fat 14 g; **Carbohydrate 4 g**; Dietary Fibre 4 g; Cholesterol 0 mg; 850 kJ (205 cal)

Green Tofu Curry

Curry Paste
10 small fresh green chillies
50 g (1¾ oz) red Asian shallots, peeled
2 cloves garlic
1 cup (50 g/1¾ oz) finely chopped coriander
stems and roots
1 stem lemon grass (white part only), chopped
2 tablespoons grated fresh galangal
1 tablespoon ground coriander
1 teaspoon ground cumin
1 teaspoon black peppercorns
½ teaspoon ground turmeric

1 tablespoon lime juice
2 tablespoons oil
1 onion, sliced
400 ml (13 fl oz) can coconut cream
4–5 kaffir lime leaves, torn
500 g (1 lb) firm tofu, cut into 2 cm (¾ inch) cubes
1 tablespoon lime juice
1 tablespoon shredded fresh Thai basil

PREPARATION TIME 20 minutes
TOTAL COOKING TIME 20 minutes
SERVES 6

1 To make the curry paste, place all the ingredients in a food processor and process until smooth.

2 Heat the oil in a frying pan, add the onion and cook for 5 minutes, or until soft. Add 4 tablespoons curry paste (or more for a stronger flavour) and cook, stirring, for 2 minutes. Stir in the coconut cream and 1 cup (250 ml/8 fl oz) water, and season with salt. Bring to the boil and add the kaffir lime leaves and tofu. Reduce the heat and simmer for 8 minutes, stirring often. Stir in the lime juice and Thai basil, and serve.

Note
The recipe for the curry paste makes 1 cup, but you will only need ⅓ cup. Freeze the remaining paste in two portions to use at a later date.

NUTRITION PER SERVE Protein 3.5 g; Fat 25 g; **Carbohydrate 3 g**; Dietary Fibre 1.5 g; Cholesterol 0 mg; 1020 kJ (242 cal)

Cauliflower Curry

Marinade
1 large onion, roughly chopped
1 teaspoon grated fresh ginger
2 cloves garlic, crushed
3 green chillies, chopped
1/4 cup (60 g/2 oz) plain yoghurt

1 cauliflower, divided into florets
oil, for deep-frying

Curry sauce
2 tablespoons ghee
1 onion, finely chopped
2 tablespoons tomato paste
2 tablespoons cream
1 teaspoon chilli powder
1 1/2 tablespoons garam masala

PREPARATION TIME 20 minutes + 30 minutes marinating
TOTAL COOKING TIME 20 minutes
SERVES 6

1 To make the marinade, place all the ingredients in a food processor and mix until smooth. Place the marinade in a bowl, add the cauliflower, toss to coat and leave for 30 minutes.

2 Fill a deep heavy-based saucepan one-third full of oil and heat to 160°C (315°F), or until a cube of bread dropped into the oil browns in 30–35 seconds. Cook the cauliflower in batches for 30 seconds until golden brown all over. Drain on paper towels.

3 Heat the ghee in a frying pan, add the onion and cook for 4–5 minutes, or until soft. Add the tomato paste, cream, chilli powder, garam masala, 1 1/2 cups (375 ml/12 fl oz) water and salt to taste. Cook, stirring constantly, over medium heat for 3 minutes.

4 Add the cauliflower and cook for 7 minutes, adding a little water if the sauce becomes dry.

NUTRITION PER SERVE Protein 2.5 g; Fat 9 g; **Carbohydrate 4.5 g**; Dietary Fibre 2 g; Cholesterol 27 mg; 458 kJ (110 cal)

Lemon Grass Prawn Satays

1 tablespoon oil
1 clove garlic, crushed
1 tablespoon grated fresh ginger
1 tablespoon finely chopped lemon grass, white part only
1 onion, finely chopped
1 tablespoon tandoori curry paste
4 kaffir lime leaves, finely shredded
1 tablespoon coconut cream

2 teaspoons grated lime rind
600 g (1 $\frac{1}{4}$ lb) raw prawns, peeled and deveined
3 stalks lemon grass, cut into 15 cm (6 inch) lengths

PREPARATION TIME 20 minutes + 1 hour refrigeration
TOTAL COOKING TIME 15 minutes
SERVES 6

1 Heat the oil in a frying pan, add the garlic, ginger, lemon grass and onion and cook over medium heat for 3 minutes, or until golden.

2 Add the tandoori paste and kaffir lime leaves to the pan and cook for 5 minutes, or until the tandoori paste is fragrant. Allow to cool slightly. Transfer the mixture to a food processor, add the coconut cream, lime rind and prawns and process until finely minced.

3 Divide the mixture into six portions and shape around the lemon grass stems with wet hands, leaving about 3 cm (1 $\frac{1}{4}$ inches) uncovered at each end of the stems. The mixture is quite soft, so take care when handling it. Using wet hands will make the mixture easier to manage. Refrigerate for 1 hour.

4 Cook the satays under a preheated medium grill for 5 minutes, or until cooked through.

NUTRITION PER SERVE Protein 20 g; Fat 5 g; **Carbohydrate 2 g**; Dietary Fibre 0 g; Cholesterol 150 mg; 500 kJ (135 cal)

Chargrilled Thai-spiced Baby Octopus

500 g (1 lb) baby octopus
2 tablespoons oil
3 cloves garlic, chopped
1 tablespoon green or pink peppercorns
2–4 small red chillies, finely chopped
1 tablespoon fish sauce

PREPARATION TIME 1 hour + 30 minutes marinating
TOTAL COOKING TIME 20 minutes
SERVES 6 as a starter

1 Use a small sharp knife to remove the octopus gut by either cutting off the head entirely or by slicing open the head and removing the gut.

2 Pick up the body and use your index finger to push up the beak. Remove the beak and discard. Clean the octopus thoroughly. Cut the head into two or three pieces. Place in a shallow dish.

3 Combine the octopus, oil, garlic, peppercorns and chilli in a bowl and marinate for 30 minutes. Heat a barbecue plate or chargrill pan until very hot. Cook three octopus at a time, turning frequently, for 3 minutes or until they turn white. Do not overcook. Sprinkle the fish sauce over the top and serve immediately.

Variation
Also suitable for calamari. Wash the tubes, pat them dry and cut them into squares or long strips, then continue as for the octopus. Don't overcook or they will be tough.

NUTRITION PER SERVE Protein 15 g; Fat 8 g; **Carbohydrate 0.5 g**; Dietary Fibre 0 g; Cholesterol 166 mg; 520 kJ (120 cal)

Mussels with Lemon Grass, Basil and Wine

1 kg (2 lb) black mussels
1 tablespoon oil
1 onion, chopped
4 cloves garlic, chopped
2 stems lemon grass, white part only, chopped
1–2 teaspoons chopped small red chillies
1 cup (250 ml/8 fl oz) white wine

1 tablespoon fish sauce
1 cup (30 g/1 oz) Thai basil leaves,
roughly chopped

PREPARATION TIME 30 minutes
TOTAL COOKING TIME 15 minutes
SERVES 4–6

1 Scrub the mussels and debeard. Soak them in a bowl of cold water for 10 minutes; drain and discard any that are open and don't close when tapped on the work surface.

2 Heat the oil in a wok and stir-fry the onion, garlic, lemon grass and chilli over low heat for 4 minutes. Add the wine and fish sauce and cook for 3 minutes.

3 Add the mussels to the wok and toss well. Cover the wok; increase the heat and cook for 3–4 minutes or until the mussels open. Discard any that don't open. Add the chopped basil and toss well before serving.

Hint

Do not overcook the mussels or they will become tough. Use small fresh black mussels and buy a few extra, in case any are cracked, damaged or already open.

NUTRITION PER SERVE Protein 13 g; Fat 5 g; **Carbohydrate 1.5 g**; Dietary Fibre 0 g; Cholesterol 30 mg; 1271 kJ (302 cal)

Japanese-style Salmon Parcels

2 teaspoons sesame seeds
4 x 150 g (5 oz) salmon cutlets or steaks
2½ cm (1 inch) piece fresh ginger
2 celery sticks
4 spring onions
¼ teaspoon dashi granules

3 tablespoons mirin
2 tablespoons tamari

PREPARATION TIME 40 minutes
TOTAL COOKING TIME 15 minutes
SERVES 4

1 Cut 4 squares of baking paper large enough to enclose the salmon steaks. Preheat the oven to very hot 230°C (450°F/Gas 8). Lightly toast the sesame seeds under a hot grill for 1 minute.

2 Wash the salmon and dry with paper towels. Place a salmon cutlet in the centre of each paper square.

3 Cut the ginger into paper-thin slices. Slice the celery and spring onions into short lengths, then lengthways into fine strips. Arrange a bundle of celery and spring onion and several slices of ginger on each salmon steak.

4 Combine the dashi granules, mirin and tamari in a small saucepan. Heat gently until the granules dissolve. Drizzle over each parcel, sprinkle with sesame seeds and carefully wrap the salmon, folding in the sides to seal in all the juices. Arrange the parcels on a baking tray and cook for about 12 minutes, or until tender. (The paper will puff up when the fish is cooked.) Do not overcook or the salmon will dry out. Serve immediately, as standing time can spoil the fish.

NUTRITION PER SERVE Protein 20 g; Fat 14 g; **Carbohydrate 0 g**; Dietary Fibre 0.5 g; Cholesterol 85 mg; 935 kJ (225 cal). NOTE Rice shown as a serving suggestion. Carbohydrate content not included in nutrition per serve.

Sesame-coated Tuna with Coriander Salsa

4 tuna steaks
³/₄ cup (120 g/4 oz) sesame seeds
100 g (3¹/₂ oz) baby rocket leaves

Coriander salsa
2 tomatoes, seeded and diced
1 large clove garlic, crushed
2 tablespoons finely chopped fresh coriander
leaves

2 tablespoons virgin olive oil, plus extra for
shallow-frying
1 tablespoon lime juice

PREPARATION TIME 15 minutes + 15 minutes
refrigeration
TOTAL COOKING TIME 10 minutes
SERVES 4

1 Cut each tuna steak into three pieces. Place the sesame seeds on a sheet of baking paper. Roll the tuna in the sesame seeds to coat. Refrigerate for 15 minutes.

2 To make the salsa, mix together the tomato, garlic, coriander, oil and lime juice. Cover and refrigerate.

3 Fill a heavy-based frying pan to 1.5 cm (⁵/₈ inch) deep with the extra oil and place over high heat. Add the tuna in two batches and cook for 2 minutes each side (it should be pink in the centre). Remove and drain on paper towels. Divide the rocket among four serving plates, top with the tuna and serve with the salsa.

NUTRITION PER SERVE Protein 26 g; Fat 36 g; **Carbohydrate 2 g**; Dietary Fibre 2 g; Cholesterol 45 mg; 1696 kJ (403 cal)

Fish with Ginger

1 tablespoon peanut oil
1 small onion, finely sliced
3 teaspoons ground coriander
600 g (1 1/4 lb) boneless white fish fillets,
such as perch, sliced
1 tablespoon julienned fresh ginger
1 teaspoon finely chopped and seeded green chilli

2 tablespoons lime juice
2 tablespoons coriander leaves

PREPARATION TIME 20 minutes
TOTAL COOKING TIME 15 minutes
SERVES 4

1 Heat a wok until very hot, add the oil and swirl to coat. Add the onion and stir-fry for 4 minutes, or until soft and golden. Add the ground coriander and cook for 1–2 minutes, or until the mixture is fragrant.

2 Add the fish, ginger and chilli, and stir-fry for 5–7 minutes, or until the fish is cooked through. Stir in the lime juice and season. Garnish with the coriander leaves and serve.

NUTRITION PER SERVE Protein 30 g; Fat 9 g; **Carbohydrate 1 g**; Dietary Fibre 0.4 g; Cholesterol 105 mg; 895 kJ (214 cal)
NOTE Rice shown as a serving suggestion. Carbohydrate content not included in nutrition per serve.

Balinese Seafood Curry

Curry Paste
2 tomatoes, peeled, seeded and roughly chopped
5 small fresh red chillies, seeded and chopped
5 cloves garlic, chopped
2 stems lemon grass (white part only), sliced
1 tablespoon coriander seeds, dry-roasted and ground
1 teaspoon shrimp powder, dry-roasted (see NOTE)
1 tablespoon ground almonds
1/4 teaspoon ground nutmeg
1 teaspoon ground turmeric
3 tablespoons tamarind purée

1 tablespoon lime juice
250 g (8 oz) swordfish, cut into 3 cm (1 1/4 inch) cubes

1/4 cup (60 ml/2 fl oz) oil
2 red onions, chopped
2 small fresh red chillies, seeded and sliced
400 g (13 oz) raw medium prawns, peeled and deveined, tails intact
250 g (8 oz) calamari tubes, cut into 1 cm (1/2 inch) rings
1/2 cup (125 ml/4 fl oz) fish stock
fresh Thai basil leaves, shredded, to garnish

PREPARATION TIME 20 minutes + 20 minutes marinating
TOTAL COOKING TIME 20 minutes
SERVES 6

1 To make the curry paste, place all the ingredients in a blender or food processor, and blend to a thick paste.

2 Place the lime juice in a bowl and season with salt and freshly ground black pepper. Add the swordfish, toss to coat well and leave to marinate for 20 minutes.

3 Heat the oil in a saucepan or wok, add the onion, sliced red chilli and curry paste, and cook, stirring occasionally, over low heat for 10 minutes, or until fragrant. Add the swordfish and prawns, and stir to coat in the curry paste mixture. Cook for 3 minutes, or until the prawns just turn pink, then add the calamari and cook for 1 minute.

4 Add the stock and bring to the boil, then reduce the heat and simmer for 2 minutes, or until the seafood is cooked and tender. Season to taste with salt and freshly ground black pepper. Garnish with the shredded fresh basil leaves.

Note
If you cannot purchase shrimp powder, place some dried baby shrimp in a mortar and pestle and grind to a fine powder. Alternatively, you can place them in the small bowl of a food processor and process to a fine powder.

NUTRITION PER SERVE Protein 30 g; Fat 14 g; **Carbohydrate 3.5 g**; Dietary Fibre 2 g; Cholesterol 210 mg; 1100 kJ (263 cal)

Creamy Garlic Seafood Stew

12 scallops, with roe
500 g (1 lb) skinless firm white fish fillets (see NOTE)
6 raw Balmain bugs or crabs
500 g (1 lb) raw medium prawns
50 g (1¾ oz) butter
1 onion, finely chopped
5–6 large cloves garlic, finely chopped
½ cup (125 ml/4 fl oz) white wine

2 cups (500 ml/16 fl oz) cream
1½ tablespoons Dijon mustard
2 teaspoons lemon juice
2 tablespoons chopped fresh flat-leaf parsley

PREPARATION TIME 20 minutes
TOTAL COOKING TIME 20 minutes
SERVES 6

1 Slice or pull off any membrane or hard muscle from the scallops. Cut the fish into 2 cm (¾ inch) cubes. Cut the heads off the bugs, then use kitchen scissors to cut down around the sides of the tail so you can flap open the shell. Remove the flesh in one piece, then slice each piece in half. Peel and devein the prawns. Refrigerate all the seafood, covered, until ready to use.

2 Melt the butter in a frying pan and cook the onion and garlic over medium heat for 2 minutes, or until the onion is softened (be careful not to burn the garlic—it may turn bitter).

3 Add the wine to the pan and cook for 4 minutes, or until reduced by half. Stir in the cream, mustard and lemon juice, and simmer for 5–6 minutes, or until reduced to almost half.

4 Add the prawns to the pan and cook for 1 minute, then add the bug meat and cook for another minute, or until white. Add the fish and cook for 2 minutes, or until cooked through (the flesh will flake easily when tested with a fork). Finally, add the scallops and cook for 1 minute. If any of the seafood is still not cooked, cook for another minute or so, but be careful not to overcook as this will result in tough flesh. Remove the frying pan from the heat and toss the parsley through. Season to taste.

Note
Try using perch, ling, bream, tuna or blue-eye.

NUTRITION PER SERVE Protein 39 g; Fat 46 g; **Carbohydrate 4 g**; Dietary Fibre 1 g; Cholesterol 316 mg; 2460 kJ (585 cal)

Lemon Chilli Chicken

2 cloves garlic, chopped
1 tablespoon grated fresh ginger
2 tablespoons olive oil
600 g (1¼ lb) chicken thigh fillets
1 teaspoon ground coriander
2 teaspoons ground cumin
½ teaspoon ground turmeric
1 chopped red chilli

½ cup (125 ml/4 fl oz) lemon juice
¾ cup (185 ml/6 fl oz) white wine
1 cup (30 g/1 oz) fresh coriander leaves

PREPARATION TIME 20 minutes
TOTAL COOKING TIME 35 minutes
SERVES 4

1 Blend the garlic, ginger and 1 tablespoon water into a paste in a small food processor or mortar and pestle. Heat the olive oil in a heavy-based pan and brown the chicken in batches. Remove and set aside.

2 Add the garlic paste to the pan and cook, stirring, for 1 minute. Add the coriander, cumin, turmeric and chilli and stir-fry for 1 minute more. Stir in the lemon juice and wine.

3 Add the chicken pieces to the pan. Bring to the boil, reduce the heat, cover and cook for 20–25 minutes, stirring occasionally, until the chicken is tender. Uncover and cook the sauce over high heat for 5 minutes to reduce it by half. Stir in the coriander and season to taste.

NUTRITION PER SERVE Protein 30 g; Fat 15 g; **Carbohydrate 0 g**; Dietary Fibre 0 g; Cholesterol 105 mg; 1290 kJ (310 cal)
NOTE Rice shown as a serving suggestion. Carbohydrate content not included in nutrition per serve.

Spicy Chicken Patties

500 g (1 lb) chicken mince
4 spring onions, finely chopped
1/3 cup (20 g/3/4 oz) finely chopped fresh
coriander leaves
2 cloves garlic, crushed
3/4 teaspoon cayenne pepper
1 egg white, lightly beaten

1 tablespoon oil
1 lemon, halved

PREPARATION TIME 10 minutes + 20 minutes
refrigeration
TOTAL COOKING TIME 10 minutes
SERVES 4

1 Preheat the oven to warm 170°C (325°F/Gas 2–3). Mix together all the ingredients except the oil and lemon, season with salt and pepper and shape the mixture into 4 patties. Refrigerate for 20 minutes before cooking.

2 Heat the oil in a large frying pan over medium heat, add the patties and cook for about 5 minutes on each side, or until browned and cooked through.

3 Squeeze the lemon on the cooked patties and drain well on paper towels.

NUTRITION PER SERVE Protein 25 g; Fat 12 g; **Carbohydrate 1 g**; Dietary Fibre 1 g; Cholesterol 105 mg; 895 kJ (215 cal)
NOTE Bread shown as a serving suggestion. Carbohydrate content not included in nutrition per serve.

Chicken and Asparagus Stir-fry

1 tablespoon oil
1 clove garlic, crushed
10 cm (4 inch) piece fresh ginger, peeled and thinly sliced
3 chicken breast fillets, sliced
4 spring onions, sliced
200 g (6½ oz) fresh asparagus spears, cut into short pieces

2 tablespoons soy sauce
⅓ cup (40 g/1¼ oz) slivered almonds, roasted

PREPARATION TIME 15 minutes
TOTAL COOKING TIME 10 minutes
SERVES 4

1 Heat a wok or large frying pan over high heat, add the oil and swirl to coat. Add the garlic, ginger and chicken and stir-fry for 1–2 minutes, or until the chicken changes colour.

2 Add the spring onion and asparagus and stir-fry for a further 2 minutes, or until the spring onion is soft.

3 Stir in the soy sauce and ¼ cup (60 ml/2 fl oz) water, cover and simmer for 2 minutes, or until the chicken is tender and the vegetables are slightly crisp. Sprinkle with the almonds.

NUTRITION PER SERVE Protein 22 g; Fat 12 g; **Carbohydrate 2 g**; Dietary Fibre 2 g; Cholesterol 39 mg; 855 kJ (204 cal)

Stir-fried Chicken Pasta

270 g (9 oz) jar sun-dried tomatoes in oil
500 g (1 lb) chicken breast fillets,
cut into thin strips
2 cloves garlic, crushed
½ cup (125 ml/4 fl oz) cream
2 tablespoons shredded basil

400 g (13 oz) penne pasta, cooked
2 tablespoons pine nuts, toasted

PREPARATION TIME 20 minutes
TOTAL COOKING TIME 15 minutes
SERVES 4–6

1 Drain the sun-dried tomatoes, reserving the oil. Thinly slice the sun-dried tomatoes.

2 Heat the wok until very hot, add 1 tablespoon of the oil reserved from the sun-dried tomatoes and swirl it around to coat the side. Stir-fry the chicken strips in batches, adding more oil when necessary.

3 Return all the chicken strips to the wok and add the garlic, sun-dried tomatoes and cream. Simmer gently for 4–5 minutes.

4 Stir in the basil and pasta, and heat through. Season well. Serve topped with the toasted pine nuts.

NUTRITION PER SERVE Protein 30 g; Fat 30 g; **Carbohydrate 5 g**; Dietary Fibre 4 g; Cholesterol 70 mg; 2696 kJ (640 cal)

Chicken with Balsamic Vinegar

2 tablespoons olive oil
8 (1.2 kg/2 lb 6½ oz) chicken pieces
½ cup (125 ml/4 fl oz) chicken stock
½ cup (125 ml/4 fl oz) dry white wine
½ cup (125 ml/4 fl oz) balsamic vinegar
40 g (1¼ oz) chilled butter

PREPARATION TIME 5 minutes
TOTAL COOKING TIME 50 minutes
SERVES 4

1 Heat the oil in a large casserole dish over medium heat and cook the chicken, in batches, for 7–8 minutes, or until browned. Pour off any excess fat.

2 Add the stock, bring to the boil, then reduce the heat and simmer, covered, for 30 minutes, or until the chicken is cooked through.

3 Add the white wine and vinegar and increase the heat to high. Boil for 1 minute, or until the liquid has thickened. Remove from the heat, stir in the butter until melted, and season. Spoon the sauce over the chicken to serve.

Note
Use a good-quality balsamic vinegar, as the cheaper varieties can be too acidic.

NUTRITION PER SERVE Protein 40 g; Fat 25 g; **Carbohydrate 0.5 g**; Dietary Fibre 0 g; Cholesterol 165 mg; 1790 kJ (430 cal)

Chicken Wrapped in Prosciutto and Sage

4 chicken breast fillets
1 tablespoon lemon juice
1 tablespoon olive oil
2 garlic cloves, bruised and halved
3 large sage leaves, shredded
8 prosciutto slices

16 sage leaves (preferably small to medium)
2 tablespoons olive oil

PREP TIME 10 minutes + 30 minutes marinating
COOKING TIME 10 minutes
SERVES 4

1 Trim the chicken of excess fat and sinew and place in a glass or ceramic bowl or dish that will hold the chicken in a single layer. Don't use metal or plastic dishes. Mix the lemon juice, olive oil, garlic and shredded sage in a small bowl, add to the chicken and stir the chicken around to make sure it is coated all over with the marinade. Cover and marinate for 30 minutes.

2 Discard the garlic and lightly season the chicken with salt and freshly ground black pepper. Wrap 2 slices of prosciutto around each breast fillet, tucking in 2 sage leaves on each side as you go. Make sure the leaves are secure, but not completely covered by the prosciutto. Secure the prosciutto with toothpicks. Using the heel of your hand, gently pound the breasts to flatten them slightly to ensure even cooking.

3 Heat the oil in a heavy-based frying pan over medium heat and cook the breasts for 5 minutes each side, or until golden and cooked through. Leave the chicken to rest for a few minutes, then remove the toothpicks and serve.

NUTRITION PER SERVE Fat 29.5 g; **Carbohydrate 0.5 g**; Protein 69 g; Dietary Fibre 0.5 g; Cholesterol 211 mg; 2285 kJ (545 Cal)

Chicken Curry Laksa

Laksa paste
1 large onion, roughly chopped
5 cm (2 inch) piece fresh ginger, chopped
8 cm (3 inch) piece galangal, peeled and chopped
1 stem lemon grass, white part only, roughly chopped
2 cloves garlic
1 fresh red chilli, seeded and diced
2 teaspoons vegetable oil
2 tablespoons mild curry paste

500 g (1 lb) chicken breast fillets, cut into cubes
2 cups (500 ml/16 fl oz) chicken stock
60 g (2 oz) rice vermicelli
50 g (1¾ oz) dried egg noodles
400 ml (13 fl oz) light coconut milk
10 snow peas, halved
3 spring onions, finely chopped
1 cup (90 g/3 oz) bean sprouts
½ cup (15 g/½ oz) fresh coriander leaves

PREPARATION TIME 30 minutes
TOTAL COOKING TIME 25 minutes
SERVES 4

1 To make the laksa paste, process the onion, ginger, galangal, lemon grass, garlic and chilli in a food processor until finely chopped. Add the oil and process until the mixture has a paste-like consistency. Spoon into a large wok, add the curry paste and stir over low heat for 1–2 minutes, until aromatic. Take care not to burn.

2 Increase the heat to medium, add the chicken and stir for 2 minutes, or until the chicken is well coated. Stir in the chicken stock and mix well. Bring slowly to the boil, then simmer for 10 minutes, or until the chicken is cooked through.

3 Meanwhile, cut the vermicelli into shorter lengths. Cook the vermicelli and egg noodles separately in large pans of boiling water for 5 minutes each. Drain and rinse in cold water.

4 Just prior to serving, add the light coconut milk and snow peas to the chicken and heat through. To serve, divide the vermicelli and noodles among four warmed serving bowls. Pour the hot laksa over the top and garnish with the spring onion, bean sprouts and coriander leaves.

Hint
If you prefer a more fiery laksa, use a medium or hot brand of curry paste or increase the amount of chillies in your laksa paste.

NUTRITION PER SERVE Protein 30 g; Fat 8 g; **Carbohydrate 4.5 g**; Dietary Fibre 3 g; Cholesterol 65 mg; 945 kJ (225 cal)

Balti Chicken

1 kg (2 lb) chicken thigh fillets
⅓ cup (80 ml/2¾ fl oz) oil
1 large red onion, finely chopped
4–5 cloves garlic, finely chopped
1 tablespoon grated fresh ginger
2 teaspoons ground cumin
2 teaspoons ground coriander
1 teaspoon ground turmeric
½ teaspoon chilli powder
425 g (14 oz) can chopped tomatoes

1 green capsicum, cut into 3 cm (1¼ inch) cubes
1–2 small fresh green chillies, seeded and finely chopped
⅓ cup (20 g/¾ oz) chopped fresh coriander
2 chopped spring onions, to garnish

PREPARATION TIME 25 minutes
TOTAL COOKING TIME 1 hour
SERVES 6

1 Remove any excess fat or sinew from the chicken thigh fillets and cut into 4–5 pieces.

2 Heat a large wok over high heat, add the oil and swirl to coat the side. Add the onion and stir-fry over medium heat for 5 minutes, or until softened but not browned. Add the garlic and ginger, and stir-fry for 3 minutes.

3 Add the spices, 1 teaspoon salt and ¼ cup (60 ml/2 fl oz) water. Increase the heat to high and stir-fry for 2 minutes, or until the mixture has thickened. Take care not to burn.

4 Add the tomato and 1 cup (250 ml/8 fl oz) water and cook, stirring often, for a further 10 minutes, or until the mixture is thick and pulpy and the oil comes to the surface.

5 Add the chicken to the wok, reduce the heat and simmer, stirring often, for 15 minutes. Add the capsicum and chilli, and simmer for 25 minutes, or until the chicken is tender. Add a little water if the mixture is too thick. Stir in the coriander and garnish with the spring onion.

Note
This curry is traditionally cooked in a Karahi or Balti pan, which is a round-bottomed, cast-iron, two-handled dish. A wok makes a good substitute.

NUTRITION PER SERVE Protein 40 g; Fat 17 g; **Carbohydrate 5 g**; Dietary Fibre 2 g; Cholesterol 83 mg; 1370 kJ (327 cal)

Pork Rolls with Roasted Capsicum

Sauce
¾ cup (185 ml/6 fl oz) beef stock
2 teaspoons soy sauce
2 tablespoons red wine
2 teaspoons wholegrain mustard
2 teaspoons cornflour

1 red capsicum
4 x 150 g (5 oz) lean pork leg steaks
⅓ cup (90 g/3 oz) ricotta

2 spring onions, finely chopped
1 clove garlic, crushed
75 g (2½ oz) rocket
4 small lean slices prosciutto (about 35 g/1¼ oz)
cooking oil spray

PREPARATION TIME 40 minutes
TOTAL COOKING TIME 30 minutes
SERVES 4

1 To make the sauce, put the beef stock, soy sauce, red wine and mustard in a pan. Blend the cornflour with 1 tablespoon water and add to the pan. Stir until the mixture boils.

2 Cut the capsicum into quarters and remove the seeds and membrane. Grill until the skin blisters and blackens. Cool under a damp tea towel, peel and cut the flesh into thin strips.

3 Flatten each steak into a thin square between 2 sheets of plastic, using a rolling pin or mallet. Combine the ricotta, onion and garlic in a bowl, then spread evenly over the pork. Top with a layer of rocket and prosciutto.

4 Place a quarter of the capsicum at one end and roll up to enclose the capsicum. Tie with string or secure with toothpicks at even intervals.

5 Spray a non-stick pan with oil and fry the pork rolls over medium heat for 5 minutes, or until well browned. Add the sauce to the pan and simmer over low heat for 10–15 minutes, or until the rolls are cooked. Remove the string or toothpicks. Slice and serve with the sauce.

NUTRITION PER SERVE Protein 40 g; Fat 5 g; **Carbohydrate 3.5 g**; Dietary Fibre 1 g; Cholesterol 95 mg; 925 kJ (220 cal)

Pork Vindaloo

¼ cup (60 ml/2 fl oz) oil
1 kg (2 lb) pork fillets, cut into bite-size pieces
2 onions, finely chopped
4 cloves garlic, finely chopped
1 tablespoon finely chopped fresh ginger
1 tablespoon garam masala

2 teaspoons brown mustard seeds
4 tablespoons vindaloo paste

PREPARATION TIME 20 minutes
TOTAL COOKING TIME 2 hours
SERVES 4

1 Heat the oil in a saucepan, add the pork in small batches and cook over medium heat for 5–7 minutes, or until browned. Remove from the pan.

2 Add the onion, garlic, ginger, garam masala and mustard seeds to the pan, and cook, stirring, for 5 minutes, or until the onion is soft.

3 Return all the meat to the pan, add the vindaloo paste and cook, stirring, for 2 minutes. Add 2½ cups (625 ml/21 fl oz) water and bring to the boil. Reduce the heat and simmer, covered, for 1½ hours, or until the meat is tender. Serve with boiled rice and pappadums.

NUTRITION PER SERVE Protein 58 g; Fat 20 g; **Carbohydrate 4 g**; Dietary Fibre 2 g; Cholesterol 125 mg; 1806 kJ (430 cal)

Pork and Coriander Stew

1 ½ tablespoons coriander seeds
800 g (1 lb 10 oz) pork fillet, cut into
2 cm (¾ inch) cubes
1 tablespoon plain flour
¼ cup (60 ml/2 fl oz) olive oil
1 large onion, thinly sliced
1 ½ cups (375 ml/12 fl oz) red wine
1 cup (250 ml/8 fl oz) chicken stock

1 teaspoon sugar
sprigs fresh coriander, to garnish

PREPARATION TIME 15 minutes + overnight
marinating
TOTAL COOKING TIME 1 hour 20 minutes
SERVES 4–6

1 Crush the coriander seeds in a mortar and pestle. Combine the pork, crushed seeds and ½ teaspoon cracked pepper in a bowl. Cover and marinate overnight in the refrigerator.

2 Combine the flour and pork, and toss to coat. Heat 2 tablespoons of the oil in a saucepan and cook the pork in batches over high heat for 1–2 minutes, or until brown. Remove.

3 Heat the remaining oil, add the onion and cook over medium heat for 2–3 minutes, or until just golden. Return the meat to the pan, add the red wine, stock and sugar, and season. Bring to the boil, then reduce the heat and simmer, covered, for 1 hour.

4 Remove the meat. Return the pan to the heat and boil over high heat for 3–5 minutes, or until the liquid is reduced and slightly thickened. Pour over the meat and top with coriander.

NUTRITION PER SERVE Protein 30 g; Fat 12 g; **Carbohydrate 2.5 g**; Dietary Fibre 0 g; Cholesterol 65 mg; 1180 kJ (282 cal)

Satay Lamb

oil, for cooking
500 g (1 lb) lamb fillet, thinly sliced
1 onion, chopped
2 cloves garlic, crushed
2 teaspoons grated fresh ginger
1–2 red chillies, seeded and finely chopped
1 teaspoon ground cumin
1 teaspoon ground coriander

$1/2$ cup (125 g/4 oz) crunchy peanut butter
1 tablespoon soy sauce
2 tablespoons lemon juice
$1/2$ cup (125 ml/4 fl oz) coconut cream

PREPARATION TIME 20 minutes
TOTAL COOKING TIME 15 minutes
SERVES 4–6

1 Heat the wok until very hot, add 1 tablespoon oil and swirl it around to coat the side. Stir-fry the lamb in batches over high heat until it is well browned and cooked, adding more oil when necessary. Remove the lamb from the wok and set aside.

2 Reheat the wok, add 1 tablespoon of the oil and stir-fry the onion over medium heat for 2–3 minutes, or until soft and transparent. Stir in the garlic, ginger, chilli, cumin and coriander, and cook for 1 minute.

3 Stir in the peanut butter, soy sauce, lemon juice, coconut cream and $1/2$ cup (125 ml/4 fl oz) water. Slowly bring to the boil. Return the lamb to the wok and stir until heated through.

NUTRITION PER SERVE Protein 25 g; Fat 25 g; **Carbohydrate 5 g**; Dietary Fibre 3 g; Cholesterol 55 mg; 1390 kJ (330 cal)

Lamb Shanks with Garlic

6 large lamb shanks
1 tablespoon oil
2 leeks, sliced
1 sprig fresh rosemary
1 cup (250 ml/8 fl oz) dry white wine
1 bulb garlic
oil, for brushing

PREPARATION TIME 20 minutes
TOTAL COOKING TIME 1 hour 25 minutes
SERVES 6

1 Preheat the oven to moderate 180°C (350°F/Gas 4). Season the lamb shanks. Heat the oil in a frying pan over medium–high heat. Cook the lamb shanks quickly in batches until well browned. Drain on paper towels, then place in a casserole dish.

2 Cook the leek in the frying pan until tender. Add to the lamb shanks with the rosemary and wine.

3 Cut the garlic horizontally through the centre. Brush the cut surfaces with a little oil. Place cut-side up in the casserole, but not covered by liquid. Bake, covered, for 1 hour. Remove the lid and bake for a further 15 minutes. Discard the rosemary. Serve with steamed vegetables.

NUTRITION PER SERVE Protein 33 g; Fat 18 g; **Carbohydrate 2 g**; Dietary Fibre 2 g; Cholesterol 101 mg; 1350 kJ (320 cal)

Lamb Korma

2 kg (4 lb) leg of lamb, boned
1 onion, chopped
2 teaspoons grated fresh ginger
3 cloves garlic
2 teaspoons ground coriander
2 teaspoons ground cumin
1 teaspoon cardamom seeds
large pinch cayenne pepper
2 tablespoons ghee or oil
1 onion, extra, sliced

2½ tablespoons tomato paste
½ cup (125 g/4 oz) plain yoghurt
½ cup (125 ml/4 fl oz) coconut cream
½ cup (50 g/1¾ oz) ground almonds
toasted slivered almonds, to serve

PREPARATION TIME 30 minutes + 1 hour marinating
TOTAL COOKING TIME 1 hour 10 minutes
SERVES 4–6

1 Trim any excess fat or sinew from the lamb, cut it into 3 cm (1¼ inch) cubes and place in a large bowl.

2 Place the chopped onion, grated ginger, garlic, ground coriander, ground cumin, cardamom seeds, cayenne pepper and ½ teaspoon salt in a food processor. Process the ingredients until they form a smooth paste. Add the spice mixture to a large bowl with the cubed lamb and mix well to coat the lamb in the spice mixture. Leave to marinate for 1 hour.

3 Heat the ghee in a large saucepan, add the sliced onion and cook, stirring, over low heat for 7 minutes, or until the onion is soft. Add the lamb and spice mixture, and cook, stirring constantly, for 8–10 minutes, or until the lamb changes colour. Stir in the tomato paste, yoghurt, coconut cream and ground almonds.

4 Reduce the heat and simmer the curry, covered, stirring occasionally, for 50 minutes, or until the meat is tender. Add a little water if the mixture becomes too dry. Season the curry with salt and pepper, and garnish with the toasted slivered almonds. Serve with steamed rice.

Note
Korma curries can also be made using beef or chicken. Korma refers to the style of curry—rich and smooth, and including almonds.

NUTRITION PER SERVe Protein 80 g; Fat 23 g; **Carbohydrate 5 g**; Dietary Fibre 2 g; Cholesterol 240 mg; 2280 kJ (545 cal)

Beef Fillet and Blue Cheese Butter

1 kg (2 lb 4 oz) beef eye fillet
1 tablespoon extra virgin olive oil
40 g (1 1/2 oz) butter
100 g (3 1/2 oz) blue castello cheese, or other
creamy blue cheese, chopped
40 g (1 1/2 oz) walnuts, roasted
1 tablespoon snipped chives
100 g (3 1/2 oz) rocket (arugula) leaves

PREPARATION TIME 10 minutes + 15 minutes
standing
COOKING TIME 30 minutes
SERVES 4

1　Preheat the oven to 210°C (415°F/Gas 6–7). Tie the beef with string to keep its shape. Heat the oil in a heavy-based frying pan, add the beef and cook, turning, for 5 minutes, or until browned all sides. Transfer to a shallow roasting tin and season with freshly ground black pepper. Bake for 25 minutes for rare beef, or until cooked to your liking. Transfer to a warm plate, cover loosely with foil and leave to rest for 10–15 minutes. Remove the string.

2　Meanwhile, put the butter in a bowl and beat until soft. Gently stir in the cheese until just combined. Finely chop half the walnuts and fold through the mixture with the chives. Form into a log and wrap in baking paper. Refrigerate until ready to use.

3　Divide the rocket leaves among four serving plates. Carve the beef into thick slices and arrange over the rocket. Cut the butter into 1/2 cm (1/4 inch) slices and arrange over the beef, sprinkle with the remaining walnuts, then serve.

NUTRITION PER SERVE Fat 40 g; **Carbohydrate 0.5 g**; Protein 60 g; Dietary Fibre 1 g; Cholesterol 220 mg; 2470 kJ (590 Cal)

Seekh Kebabs

pinch of ground cloves
pinch of ground nutmeg
$\frac{1}{2}$ teaspoon chilli powder
1 teaspoon ground cumin
2 teaspoons ground coriander
3 cloves garlic, finely chopped
5 cm (2 inch) piece of fresh ginger, grated
500 g (1 lb) lean beef mince
1 tablespoon oil
2 tablespoons lemon juice

Onion and mint relish
1 red onion, finely chopped
1 tablespoon white vinegar
1 tablespoon lemon juice
1 tablespoon chopped fresh mint

PREPARATION TIME 40 minutes
TOTAL COOKING TIME 12 minutes
SERVES 4

1 Soak 12 thick wooden skewers in cold water for 15 minutes. Dry-fry the cloves, nutmeg, chilli, cumin and coriander in a heavy-based frying pan, over low heat, for about 2 minutes, shaking the pan constantly. Transfer to a bowl with the garlic and ginger and set aside.

2 Knead the mince firmly using your fingertips and the base of your hand. The meat needs to be kneaded constantly for about 3 minutes, or until it becomes very soft and a little sticky. This process changes the texture of the meat when cooked, making it very soft and tender. Add the mince to the spice and garlic mixture and mix well, seasoning well.

3 Form tablespoons of the meat into small, round patty shapes. Wet your hands and press two portions of the meat around a skewer, leaving a

gap of about 3 cm (1$\frac{1}{4}$ inches) at the top of the skewer. Smooth the outside gently, place on baking paper and refrigerate while making the remaining kebabs.

4 To make the onion and mint relish, mix together the onion, vinegar and lemon juice and refrigerate for 10 minutes. Stir in the mint and season with pepper just before serving.

5 Grill the skewers or cook on an oiled barbecue flat plate for about 8 minutes, turning regularly and sprinkling with a little lemon juice. Serve with the relish.

Storage
These kebabs freeze very well—simply defrost before grilling.

NUTRITION PER SERVE Protein 26 g; Fat 20 g; **Carbohydrate 2 g**; Dietary Fibre 1 g; Cholesterol 80 mg; 1156 kJ (280 cal)
NOTE Rice shown as a serving suggestion. Carbohydrate content not included in nutrition per serve.

Beef with Bok Choy

1 bunch bok choy (see VARIATION)
oil, for cooking
2 cloves garlic, crushed
250 g (8 oz) rump steak, thinly sliced
2 tablespoons soy sauce
1 tablespoon sweet sherry

2 tablespoons chopped basil
2 teaspoons sesame oil

PREPARATION TIME 20 minutes
TOTAL COOKING TIME 10 minutes
SERVES 4

1 Wash the bok choy and drain. Cut the leaves into wide strips and the stems into thin strips. Heat the wok until very hot, add 1 tablespoon of the oil and swirl to coat the side. Add the garlic and stir-fry for 30 seconds.

2 Add another tablespoon of oil to the wok and add the meat in batches. Stir-fry for 3 minutes over high heat until the meat has browned but not cooked through. Remove from the wok.

3 Add the bok choy to the wok and stir-fry for 30 seconds or until just wilted. Add the meat, soy sauce and sherry. Stir-fry for 2–3 minutes or until the meat is tender.

4 Add the basil and sesame oil and toss well. Serve immediately.

Variation
The Asian vegetable, choy sum, has a similar flavour to bok choy and could also be used for this recipe. It has a longer leaf and shorter stem. Baby bok choy could also be used for this recipe.

NUTRITION PER SERVE Protein 60 g; Fat 40 g; **Carbohydrate 0.5 g**; Dietary Fibre 1 g; Cholesterol 42 mg; 790 kJ (190 cal)

Beef in Beer with Capers

1 kg (2 lb) gravy beef
seasoned plain flour
olive oil, for cooking
4 cloves garlic, finely chopped
2 cups (500 ml/16 fl oz) beef stock
1 1/2 cups (375 ml/12 fl oz) beer
2 onions, chopped
3 bay leaves

1/3 cup (55 g/2 oz) stuffed or pitted green olives,
sliced
6 anchovies
2 tablespoons capers, drained

PREPARATION TIME 25 minutes
TOTAL COOKING TIME 3 hours 20 minutes
SERVES 4–6

1 Cut the beef into 4 cm (1 1/2 inch) chunks. Lightly coat in the flour. Heat 1/4 cup (60 ml/2 fl oz) of oil in a deep heavy-based pan, add the garlic, then brown the beef over high heat.

2 Add the stock, beer, onion and bay leaves, season well and bring to the boil. Reduce the heat and gently simmer, covered, for 2 1/2 hours, stirring about three times during cooking. Remove the lid and simmer for 30 minutes more. Stir, then mix in the olives.

3 Heat 2 teaspoons of oil in a small pan. Add the anchovies and capers, gently breaking up the anchovies. Cook over medium heat for 4 minutes, or until brown and crisp. To serve, place the meat on serving plates, drizzle with the sauce, sprinkle with anchovies and capers, and season with salt and freshly cracked pepper.

Note
The capers should be squeezed very dry before being added to the pan, or they will spit in the hot oil.

NUTRITION PER SERVE Protein 40 g; Fat 6 g; **Carbohydrate 4 g**; Dietary Fibre 1 g; Cholesterol 115 mg; 965 kJ (230 cal)

Madras Beef Curry

1 tablespoon oil or ghee
1 onion, chopped
3–4 tablespoons Madras curry paste
1 kg (2 lb) skirt or chuck steak, cut into 2$\frac{1}{2}$ cm
(1 inch) cubes
$\frac{1}{4}$ cup (60 g/2 oz) tomato paste
1 cup (250 ml/8 fl oz) beef stock

PREPARATION TIME 20 minutes
TOTAL COOKING TIME 1 hour 45 minutes
SERVES 4

1 Heat the oil in a large frying pan, add the onion and cook over medium heat for 10 minutes, or until browned. Add the curry paste and stir for 1 minute, or until fragrant. Then add the meat and cook, stirring, until coated with the curry paste.

2 Stir in the tomato paste and stock. Reduce the heat and simmer, covered, for 1$\frac{1}{4}$ hours, and then uncovered for 15 minutes, or until the meat is tender.

NUTRITION PER SERVE Protein 53 g; Fat 15 g; **Carbohydrate 4.5 g**; Dietary Fibre 1.5 g; Cholesterol 170 mg; 1514 kJ (362 cal)

Mandarin Ice

10 mandarins
125 g (4 oz) caster (superfine) sugar

PREPARATION TIME 10 minutes + freezing
TOTAL COOKING TIME 10 minutes
SERVES 4–6

1 Squeeze the mandarins to make 2 cups (500 ml/ 16 fl oz) juice and strain.

2 Place the sugar and 1 cup (250 ml/8 fl oz) water in a small saucepan. Stir over low heat until the sugar has dissolved and simmer for 5 minutes. Remove from the heat and cool slightly.

3 Stir the mandarin juice into the sugar syrup, then pour into a shallow metal tray. Freeze for 2 hours, or until frozen. Transfer to a food processor and blend until slushy. Return to the freezer and repeat the process three more times.

NUTRITION PER SERVE Fat 0 g; Protein 0.5 g; **Carbohydrate 5.5 g**; Dietary Fibre 0 g; Cholesterol 0 mg; 105 kJ (25 Cal)

Spicy Coconut Custard

2 cinnamon sticks
1 teaspoon ground nutmeg
2 teaspoons whole cloves
300 ml (10 fl oz) cream
1/2 cup (125 g/4 oz) palm sugar, chopped
280 g (9 oz) can coconut milk

3 eggs, lightly beaten
2 egg yolks, lightly beaten

PREPARATION TIME 20 minutes
TOTAL COOKING TIME 1 hour
SERVES 8

1 Preheat the oven to warm 160°C (315°F/Gas 2–3). Put the spices, cream and 1 cup (250 ml/8 fl oz) water in a pan. Bring to simmering point, then reduce the heat to very low and leave for 5 minutes to allow the spices to flavour the liquid.

2 Add the sugar and coconut milk to the pan, return to low heat and stir until the sugar has dissolved.

3 Whisk the eggs and egg yolks together. Pour the spiced mixture over the eggs and stir well. Strain, discarding the whole spices. Pour the custard mixture into eight 1/2-cup (125 ml/4 fl oz) dishes. Put the dishes in a roasting tin and pour enough boiling water into the tin to come halfway up the sides of the dishes. Bake for 40–45 minutes.

4 Poke a knife in the centre of one of the custards to check if they are set—the mixture should be only slightly wobbly. Remove the custards from the roasting tin and serve hot or chilled.

Storage
The custards will keep, covered and refrigerated, for up to three days.

NUTRITION PER SERVE Protein 5 g; Fat 26 g; **Carbohydrate 3 g**; Dietary Fibre 0 g; Cholesterol 166 mg; 1080 kJ (260 cal)

Fudge Brownies

cooking oil spray
$\frac{1}{2}$ cup (60 g/2 oz) plain flour
$\frac{1}{2}$ cup (60 g/2 oz) self-raising flour
1 teaspoon bicarbonate of soda
$\frac{3}{4}$ cup (90 g/3 oz) cocoa powder
2 eggs
1$\frac{1}{4}$ cups (310 g/10 oz) caster sugar
2 teaspoons vanilla essence

2 tablespoons vegetable oil
200 g (6$\frac{1}{2}$ oz) low-fat fromage frais
140 ml (4$\frac{1}{2}$ fl oz) apple purée
icing sugar, for dusting

PREPARATION TIME 15 minutes
TOTAL COOKING TIME 30 minutes
MAKES 18 pieces

1 Preheat the oven to moderate 180°C (350°F/Gas 4). Spray a 30 x 20 cm (12 x 8 inch) shallow baking tin with oil, and line the base of the tin with baking paper.

2 Sift the flours, bicarbonate of soda and cocoa powder into a large bowl. Mix the eggs, sugar, vanilla essence, oil, fromage frais and purée in a large bowl, stirring until well combined. Add to the flour and stir until combined. Spread into the prepared tin and bake for about 30 minutes, or until a skewer inserted in the centre comes out clean.

3 The brownie will sink slightly in the centre as it cools. Leave in the pan for 5 minutes before turning onto a wire rack to cool. Dust with icing sugar before cutting into pieces to serve.

NUTRITION PER PIECE Protein 2.5 g; Fat 3.5 g; **Carbohydrate 2.5 g**; Dietary Fibre 5 g; Cholesterol 20 mg; 595 kJ (140 cal)

6–10 g

Warm Radicchio Salad with Crushed Tomato Vinaigrette

4–5 tablespoons olive oil
6 cloves garlic, thinly sliced
7 Roma (egg or plum) tomatoes, cored and halved
3 tablespoons extra virgin olive oil
2 tablespoons red wine vinegar
1 teaspoon honey
920 g (1 lb 14 oz) chicory

1 onion, halved and sliced
1 radicchio lettuce

PREPARATION TIME 40 minutes
TOTAL COOKING TIME 25 minutes
SERVES 4

1   Heat half the olive oil in a small frying pan, add the garlic and fry over moderately high heat for a few minutes, or until lightly browned. Drain on paper towels.

2   Heat a little more olive oil in the frying pan and cook the tomatoes, cut-side-down, over moderate heat until browned and very soft. Turn to brown the other side. Transfer to a bowl to cool, then peel and discard the skins. Coarsely mash the flesh with a fork.

3   To make the vinaigrette, whisk together about half of the crushed tomatoes, the extra virgin olive oil, the vinegar and the honey. Season with salt and freshly ground black pepper.

4   Trim the coarse stems from the chicory, wash the leaves very well and drain. Cut into short lengths. Heat the rest of the olive oil in the frying pan, add the onion and cook until transparent. Add the chicory and stir until just wilted. Add the remaining tomatoes and stir until well combined. Season with salt and black pepper.

5   Tear any large radicchio leaves into smaller pieces. Toss through the chicory mixture. Transfer to a large serving bowl, drizzle with the tomato vinaigrette and sprinkle with the garlic. Serve immediately.

NUTRITION PER SERVE Protein 7 g; Fat 35 g; **Carbohydrate 9 g**; Dietary Fibre 8 g; Cholesterol 0 mg; 1620 kJ (385 cal)

Lime and Prawn Salad

200 g (6$\frac{1}{2}$ oz) baby green beans
2 Lebanese cucumbers, sliced
4 spring onions, finely chopped
1 tablespoon finely shredded kaffir lime leaves
$\frac{1}{4}$ cup (15 g/$\frac{1}{2}$ oz) flaked coconut
750 g (1$\frac{1}{2}$ lb) cooked prawns, peeled, tails intact
2 teaspoons shredded lime rind

Dressing
1 tablespoon peanut oil
1 tablespoon nam pla (Thai fish sauce)
1 tablespoon grated palm sugar
1 tablespoon chopped fresh coriander
2 teaspoons soy sauce
1–2 teaspoons sweet chilli sauce
$\frac{1}{4}$ cup (60 ml/2 fl oz) lime juice

PREPARATION TIME 35 minutes
TOTAL COOKING TIME 2 minutes
SERVES 4

1 Cook the beans in a small pan of boiling water for 2 minutes. Drain and cover with cold water, then drain again and pat dry with paper towels.

2 To make the dressing, whisk the ingredients in a bowl.

3 Combine the beans, cucumber, spring onion, lime leaves, flaked coconut and prawns in a large bowl. Add the dressing and toss gently to combine. Place the salad in a large serving bowl and garnish with the shredded lime rind.

Note
Young lemon leaves can be used in place of the kaffir lime leaves if they are not available. Soft brown or dark brown sugar may be substituted for the palm sugar.

NUTRITION PER SERVE Protein 45 g; Fat 8 g; **Carbohydrate 7 g**; Dietary Fibre 3 g; Cholesterol 350 mg; 1200 kJ (285 cal)

Chargrilled Tuna and Ruby Grapefruit Salad

4 ruby grapefruit
cooking oil spray
3 tuna steaks
150 g (5 oz) rocket leaves
1 red onion, sliced

Dressing
2 tablespoons almond oil
2 tablespoons raspberry vinegar
1/2 teaspoon sugar
1 tablespoon shredded fresh mint

PREPARATION TIME 20 minutes
TOTAL COOKING TIME 10 minutes
SERVES 6

1 Cut a slice off each end of the grapefruit and peel away the skin, removing all the pith. Separate the segments and set aside in a bowl.

2 Heat a chargrill plate and spray lightly with oil. Cook each tuna steak for 3–4 minutes on each side. This will leave the centre slightly pink. Cool, then thinly slice or flake.

3 To make the dressing, put the almond oil, vinegar, sugar and mint in a small screw-top jar and shake until well combined.

4 Place the rocket on a serving plate and top with the grapefruit segments, then the tuna and onion. Drizzle with the dressing and serve.

NUTRITION PER SERVE Protein 15 g; Fat 7 g; **Carbohydrate 8 g**; Dietary Fibre 2 g; Cholesterol 50 mg; 1015 kJ (240 cal)

Tandoori Lamb Salad

1 cup (250 g/8 oz) low-fat natural yoghurt
2 cloves garlic, crushed
2 teaspoons grated fresh ginger
2 teaspoons ground turmeric
2 teaspoons garam masala
$1/4$ teaspoon paprika
2 teaspoons ground coriander
red food colouring, optional
500 g (1 lb) lean lamb fillets
4 tablespoons lemon juice

$1 1/2$ teaspoons chopped fresh coriander
1 teaspoon chopped fresh mint
150 g (5 oz) mixed salad leaves
1 large mango, cut into strips
2 cucumbers, cut into matchsticks

PREPARATION TIME 20 minutes + overnight marinating
TOTAL COOKING TIME 15 minutes
SERVES 4 as a light lunch or starter

1 Mix the yoghurt, garlic, ginger and spices in a bowl, add a little colouring and toss with the lamb to thoroughly coat. Cover and refrigerate overnight.

2 Grill the lamb on a foil-lined baking tray under high heat for 7 minutes each side, or until the marinade starts to brown. Set aside for 5 minutes before serving.

3 Mix the lemon juice, coriander and mint, then season. Toss with the salad leaves, mango and cucumber, then arrange on plates. Slice the lamb and serve over the salad.

NUTRITION PER SERVE Protein 30 g; Fat 6.5 g; **Carbohydrate 8 g**; Dietary Fibre 2 g; Cholesterol 90 mg; 965 kJ (230 cal)

Thai Beef Salad with Mint and Coriander

2 tablespoons dried shrimp
125 g (4 oz) English spinach
1 tablespoon sesame oil
500 g (1 lb) rump steak
1 cup (90 g/3 oz) bean sprouts
1 small red onion, thinly sliced
1 small red capsicum, cut into thin strips
1 small Lebanese cucumber, cut into thin strips
200 g (6½ oz) daikon radish, peeled and cut into thin strips
1 small tomato, halved, seeded and thinly sliced
¼ cup (5 g/¼ oz) mint leaves
½ cup (15 g/½ oz) coriander leaves

2 cloves garlic, finely chopped
1–2 small red chillies, chopped
2 small green chillies, chopped

Dressing
¼ cup (60 ml/2 fl oz) lime juice
¼ cup (60 ml/2 fl oz) fish sauce
1 tablespoon finely chopped lemon grass
1 teaspoon sugar

PREPARATION TIME 40 minutes
TOTAL COOKING TIME 4 minutes
SERVES 6

1 Soak the dried shrimp in hot water for 15 minutes; drain well and chop finely. Wash the English spinach and drain well. Trim the thick stalks and coarsely shred the leaves.

2 Heat the oil in a frying pan, add the steak and cook over high heat for 1½–2 minutes on each side until medium–rare. Allow to cool slightly and then slice the steak thinly.

3 To make the dressing, combine the lime juice, fish sauce, lemon grass and sugar in a small jug. Whisk until the ingredients are well combined.

4 To assemble the salad, combine the shrimp, sliced beef, bean sprouts, onion, capsicum, cucumber, radish, tomato, mint, coriander, garlic and chillies in a large bowl. Place the spinach on a serving plate, top with the combined beef and vegetables, and drizzle with the dressing.

NUTRITION PER SERVE Protein 25 g; Fat 6 g; **Carbohydrate 6 g**; Dietary Fibre 4 g; Cholesterol 65 mg; 730 kJ (175 cal)

Stuffed Zucchini

8 zucchini
35 g (1 1/4 oz) white bread, crusts removed
milk, for soaking
125 g (4 oz) ricotta cheese
3 tablespoons grated Cheddar cheese
1/3 cup (35 g/1 1/4 oz) grated Parmesan
2 teaspoons chopped fresh oregano

2 teaspoons chopped fresh thyme
1 clove garlic, crushed
1 egg yolk

PREPARATION TIME 20 minutes
TOTAL COOKING TIME 45 minutes
SERVES 4

1 Preheat the oven to moderately hot 190°C (375°F/Gas 5). Cook the zucchini in boiling salted water for 5 minutes, then drain. Meanwhile, soak the bread in milk until soft, then squeeze dry. Cut the zucchini in half and scoop out the flesh with a spoon.

2 Chop the zucchini flesh finely. Place in a bowl and add the bread, cheeses, herbs, garlic, egg yolk, and season with salt and pepper. Mix together, adding a little milk to make it bind if necessary.

3 Fill the zucchini shells with the stuffing. Brush an ovenproof baking dish with oil and arrange the zucchini close together. Bake in the oven for 35–40 minutes, until golden on top. Serve immediately.

NUTRITION PER SERVE Protein 12 g; Fat 10 g; **Carbohydrate 10 g**; Dietary Fibre 4.5 g; Cholesterol 73 mg; 758 kJ (180 cal)

Mushroom and Ricotta Filo Tart

60 g (2 oz) butter
270 g (9 oz) field mushrooms, sliced
2 cloves garlic, crushed
1 tablespoon Marsala
1 teaspoon fresh thyme leaves
1/2 teaspoon chopped fresh rosemary leaves
pinch of freshly grated nutmeg
5 sheets filo pastry
75 g (2 1/2 oz) butter, melted

200 g (6 1/2 oz) ricotta cheese
2 eggs, lightly beaten
1/2 cup (125 g/4 oz) sour cream
1 tablespoon chopped fresh parsley

PREPARATION TIME 35 minutes
TOTAL COOKING TIME 40 minutes
SERVES 6

1 Preheat the oven to 180°C (350°F/Gas 4). Melt the butter in a frying pan and add the mushrooms. Cook over high heat for a few minutes, until they begin to soften. Add the garlic and cook for another minute. Stir in the Marsala, thyme, rosemary and nutmeg. Remove the mushrooms from the pan and drain off any liquid.

2 Work with 1 sheet of filo pastry at a time, keeping the rest covered with a damp tea towel to stop them drying out. Brush the sheets with melted butter and fold in half. Place on top of each other to line a shallow 23 cm (9 inch) loose-based tart tin, allowing the edges to overhang.

3 Beat the ricotta, eggs and sour cream together and season to taste. Spoon half the mixture into the tin, then add the mushrooms. Top with the rest of the ricotta mixture. Bake for 35 minutes, or until firm. Sprinkle with the chopped parsley.

NUTRITION PER SERVE Protein 9 g; Fat 35 g; **Carbohydrate 9 g**; Dietary Fibre 2 g; Cholesterol 160 mg; 1515 kJ (360 cal)

Thai Chicken Balls

1 kg (2 lb) chicken mince
1 cup (90 g/3 oz) fresh breadcrumbs
4 spring onions, sliced
1 tablespoon ground coriander
1 cup (50 g/1¾ oz) chopped fresh coriander
3 tablespoons sweet chilli sauce

1–2 tablespoons lemon juice
2 tablespoons oil

PREPARATION TIME 20 minutes
TOTAL COOKING TIME 40 minutes
SERVES 6

1 Preheat the oven to moderately hot 200°C (400°F/Gas 6). Mix the mince and breadcrumbs in a large bowl.

2 Add the spring onion, ground and fresh coriander, chilli sauce and lemon juice and mix well. Using damp hands, form the mixture into evenly shaped balls that are either small enough to eat with your fingers or large enough to use as burgers.

3 Heat the oil in a large non-stick frying pan and cook the chicken balls over high heat until browned all over. Drain well on paper towels and then place them on a baking tray and bake until cooked through. (The small chicken balls will take 5 minutes to cook and the larger ones will take 10–15 minutes.)

NUTRITION PER SERVE Protein 40 g; Fat 8 g; **Carbohydrate 10 g**; Dietary Fibre 1 g; Cholesterol 85 mg; 1160 kJ (275 cal)

Mediterranean Ricotta Tarts

⅓ cup (30 g/1 oz) dry breadcrumbs
2 tablespoons virgin olive oil
1 clove garlic, crushed
½ red capsicum, quartered and cut into thin strips
1 zucchini, cut into thin strips
2 slices prosciutto, chopped
375 g (12 oz) firm ricotta (see NOTE)
⅓ cup (40 g/1½ oz) grated Cheddar

⅓ cup (30 g/1 oz) grated Parmesan
2 tablespoons shredded fresh basil
4 black olives, pitted and sliced

PREPARATION TIME 20 minutes + 20 minutes cooling
TOTAL COOKING TIME 30 minutes
MAKES 4

1 Preheat the oven to 180°C (350°F/Gas 4). Lightly grease four 8 cm (3 inch) fluted tart tins. Lightly sprinkle 1 teaspoon breadcrumbs over the base and side of each tin.

2 To make the topping, heat half the oil in a frying pan, add the garlic, capsicum and zucchini and cook, stirring, over medium heat for 5 minutes, or until the vegetables are soft. Remove from the heat and add the prosciutto. Season to taste.

3 Place the ricotta in a large bowl and add the cheeses and remaining breadcrumbs. Season. Press the mixture into the tins and smooth the surface. Sprinkle with basil.

4 Scatter the topping over the ricotta mixture, top with the olives, then drizzle with the remaining oil.

5 Bake for 20 minutes, or until the tarts are slightly puffed and golden. Cool completely (the tarts will deflate on cooling) and remove from the tins. Do not refrigerate.

Note
Use firm ricotta or very well-drained ricotta, or the tarts will be difficult to remove from the tins.

NUTRITION PER TART Protein 20 g; Fat 27 g; **Carbohydrate 8 g**; Dietary Fibre 1 g; Cholesterol 66 mg; 1457 kJ (348 cal)

Chinese Hot and Sour Soup

8 dried shiitake mushrooms
2 teaspoons cornflour
2 teaspoons sesame oil
1 litre (3 fl oz) vegetable stock
125 g (4 oz) bamboo shoots, cut into thin strips
125 g (4 oz) silken firm tofu, cut into long thin strips
2 teaspoons light soy sauce
3 tablespoons white wine vinegar

1/2 teaspoon white pepper
spring onions, thinly sliced, to garnish

PREPARATION TIME 15 minutes + 30 minutes soaking
TOTAL COOKING TIME 15 minutes
SERVES 4

1   Soak the mushrooms in a bowl with 1/2 cup (125 ml/4 fl oz) hot water for 30 minutes. Drain and reserve the liquid in a small bowl. Discard the stems and cut the caps into quarters.

2   Whisk the cornflour, sesame oil and 2 tablespoons of the stock together.

3   Place the remaining stock and reserved mushroom liquid in a large saucepan and bring to the boil. Add the mushrooms and bamboo shoots. Season with salt, reduce the heat and simmer for 5 minutes.

4   Add the tofu, soy sauce, vinegar and white pepper. Return the soup to a simmer. Stir in the cornflour mixture and cook until the soup thickens slightly. Pour into individual serving bowls and garnish with spring onion.

Hint

For a hotter soup, add extra white pepper before serving.

NUTRITION PER SERVE Protein 3.5 g; Fat 4 g; **Carbohydrate 6 g**; Dietary Fibre 1 g; Cholesterol 0 mg; 320 kJ (75 cal)

Chunky Chicken and Vegetable Soup

1 tablespoon oil
1 carrot, sliced
1 leek, chopped
2 chicken thigh fillets, cut into 2 cm (1 inch) pieces
1/4 cup (35 g/1 oz) ditalini pasta
4 cups (1 litre/32 fl oz) vegetable stock
2 ripe tomatoes, diced

PREPARATION TIME 15 minutes
TOTAL COOKING TIME 20 minutes
SERVES 4

1 Heat the oil in a saucepan and cook the carrot and leek over medium heat for 4 minutes, or until soft. Add the chicken and cook for a further 2 minutes, or until the chicken has changed colour.

2 Add the pasta and the vegetable stock, cover and bring to the boil. Reduce the heat and simmer for 10 minutes, or until the pasta is cooked. Add the tomato halfway through the cooking. Season to taste with salt and pepper.

Note
Ditalini pasta can be replaced with any small soup pasta.

NUTRITION PER SERVE Protein 20 g; Fat 7 g; **Carbohydrate 9 g**; Dietary Fibre 2 g; Cholesterol 40 mg; 725 kJ (173 cal)

Lemon-scented Broth with Tortellini

1 lemon
½ cup (125 ml/4 fl oz) white wine
440 g (14 oz) can chicken consommé
⅓ cup (20 g/¾ oz) chopped fresh parsley
375 g (12 oz) fresh or dried veal- or chicken-filled
tortellini

PREPARATION TIME 10 minutes
TOTAL COOKING TIME 20 minutes
SERVES 4–6

1 Using a vegetable peeler, peel wide strips from the lemon. Remove the white pith with a small sharp knife and cut three of the wide pieces into fine strips. Set these aside for garnishing.

2 Place the wide lemon strips, white wine, consommé and 3 cups (750 ml/24 fl oz) water in a large deep pan. Cook for 10 minutes over low heat. Remove the lemon rind and bring to the boil.

3 Add half the parsley, the tortellini and a sprinkling of black pepper to the pan. Cook for 6–7 minutes or until the pasta is al dente. Garnish with the remaining parsley and the fine strips of lemon.

Storage
If you want, you can prepare the recipe up to the end of step 2 and then leave in the fridge for a day before adding the pasta.

NUTRITION PER SERVE Protein 6 g; Fat 4 g; **Carbohydrate 9 g**; Dietary Fibre 2 g; Cholesterol 14 mg; 483 kJ (115 cal)

Pork Ball and Vegetable Soup

90 g (3 oz) stale white bread, crusts removed
500 g (1 lb) pork mince
2 teaspoons chopped fresh coriander roots and stems
3 teaspoons chopped fresh coriander leaves
½ teaspoon five-spice powder
1 teaspoon grated fresh ginger
1 egg white
3 cups (270 g/9 oz) bean sprouts
2 teaspoons sesame oil
2¼ litres chicken stock

1 small red chilli, chopped
2 carrots, cut into strips
2 sticks celery, cut into strips
6 spring onions, cut into strips
1½ tablespoons lime juice
coriander leaves, to serve

PREPARATION TIME 45 minutes
TOTAL COOKING TIME 10 minutes
SERVES 6–8

1 Line a baking tin with baking paper. Cover the bread with cold water, then squeeze out the liquid. Mix with the mince, coriander, five-spice powder, ginger, egg white and ¼ teaspoon each of salt and pepper.

2 Roll ½ tablespoons of the mixture into balls and lay in the lined tin. Divide the bean sprouts among bowls. Mix the sesame oil and stock in a large saucepan, bring to the boil and add the pork balls in batches. Return to the boil and, when they float, divide among the bowls.

3 Add the chilli, carrot, celery and spring onion to the stock, bring to the boil and simmer for 1 minute. Remove from the heat, season to taste and add the lime juice. Ladle into bowls and top with a few coriander leaves.

Note
Five-spice is a mixture of Sichuan pepper, star anise, fennel, cloves and cinnamon.

NUTRITION PER SERVE Protein 4 g; Fat 8 g; **Carbohydrate 10 g**; Dietary Fibre 2 g; Cholesterol 2 mg; 575 kJ (160 cal)

Hot Beef Borscht

500 g (1 lb) gravy beef, cut into large pieces
500 g (1 lb) fresh beetroot
1 onion, finely chopped
1 carrot, cut into short strips
1 parsnip, cut into short strips
1 cup (75 g/2½ oz) finely shredded cabbage
sour cream and chopped fresh chives, to serve

PREPARATION TIME 30 minutes
TOTAL COOKING TIME 2 hours 50 minutes
SERVES 4–6

1 Put the beef and 1 litre water in a large, heavy-based saucepan, and bring slowly to the boil. Reduce the heat, cover and simmer for 1 hour. Skim the surface as required.

2 Cut the stems from the beetroot, wash well and place in a large, heavy-based saucepan with 1 litre (32 fl oz) water. Bring to the boil, then reduce the heat and simmer for 40 minutes, or until tender. Drain, reserving 1 cup (250 ml/8 fl oz) of the liquid. Cool, then peel and grate the beetroot.

3 Remove the meat from the stock, cool and dice. Skim any fat from the surface of the stock. Return the meat to the stock and add the onion, carrot, parsnip, beetroot and reserved liquid. Bring to the boil, reduce the heat, cover and simmer for 45 minutes.

4 Stir in the cabbage and simmer for a further 15 minutes. Season to taste. Serve with the sour cream and chives.

NUTRITION PER SERVE Protein 20 g; Fat 10 g; **Carbohydrate 10 g**; Dietary Fibre 5 g; Cholesterol 80 mg; 940 kJ (225 cal)

Tofu Kebabs with Miso Pesto

1 large red capsicum, cut into squares
12 button mushrooms, halved
6 pickling onions, quartered
3 zucchini, thickly sliced
450 g (14 oz) firm tofu, cut into small cubes
1/2 cup (125 ml/4 fl oz) olive oil
1/4 cup (60 ml/2 fl oz) soy sauce
2 cloves garlic, crushed
2 teaspoons grated fresh ginger

Miso pesto
1/2 cup (90 g/3 oz) unsalted roasted peanuts
2 cups (60 g/2 oz) firmly packed fresh coriander leaves
2 tablespoons white miso paste
2 cloves garlic
100 ml (3 1/2 fl oz) olive oil

PREPARATION TIME 30 minutes + 1 hour marinating
TOTAL COOKING TIME 10 minutes
SERVES 4

1 Soak 12 wooden skewers in cold water for 10 minutes. Thread the vegetable pieces and tofu alternately onto the skewers, then place in a large shallow non-metallic dish.

2 Combine the olive oil, soy sauce, garlic and ginger, then pour half the mixture over the kebabs. Cover with plastic wrap and marinate for 1 hour.

3 To make the miso pesto, finely chop the peanuts, coriander leaves, miso paste and garlic in a food processor. Slowly add the olive oil while the machine is still running and blend to a smooth paste.

4 Heat a chargrill pan or barbecue grill plate and cook the kebabs, turning and brushing often with the remaining marinade, for 4–6 minutes, or until the edges are slightly brown. Serve with the miso pesto.

NUTRITION PER SERVE Protein 8 g; Fat 64 g; **Carbohydrate 10 g**; Dietary Fibre 4 g; Cholesterol 0 mg; 2698 kJ (645 cal)

Tofu with Asian Greens and Shiitake Mushrooms

⅓ cup (80 ml/2¾ fl oz) vegetable oil
1 clove garlic, chopped
1 teaspoon grated fresh ginger
60 g (2 oz) shiitake mushrooms, sliced
2 teaspoons dashi powder
3 tablespoons mushroom soy sauce
3 tablespoons mirin
1 teaspoon sugar
2 tablespoons cornflour

2 x 300 g (10 oz) blocks silken firm tofu, each
block cut into 4 slices
250 g (8 oz) bok choy, chopped
150 g (5 oz) choy sum, chopped
2 spring onions, cut on the diagonal
wasabi, to serve

PREPARATION TIME 15 minutes
TOTAL COOKING TIME 20 minutes
SERVES 4

1 Heat 1 tablespoon of the oil in a saucepan. Add the garlic, ginger and mushrooms and fry for 1–2 minutes, or until softened. Add the dashi powder and 2 cups (500 ml/16 fl oz) water and simmer for 5 minutes.

2 Add the mushroom soy sauce, mirin and sugar and stir until the sugar has dissolved. Mix the cornflour with a little water to make a smooth paste. Pour into the soy sauce mixture and stir until thickened.

3 Heat 2 tablespoons of the oil in a frying pan. Add the tofu and brown in batches for 2–3 minutes. Set aside. Heat the remaining oil, then add the bok choy, choy sum and spring onion. Cook for 2 minutes, or until wilted.

4 Place the greens in a bowl, top with the tofu and pour on the dashi sauce. Serve a little wasabi on the side.

NUTRITION PER SERVE Protein 17 g; Fat 25 g; **Carbohydrate 6 g**; Dietary Fibre 5 g; Cholesterol 0 mg; 1368 kJ (327 cal)

Eggplant Parmigiana

¼ cup (60 ml/2 fl oz) olive oil
1 onion, diced
2 cloves garlic, crushed
1 ¼ kg (2 lb 8 oz) tomatoes, peeled and chopped
oil, for shallow-frying
1 kg (2 lb) eggplants, very thinly sliced
250 g (8 oz) bocconcini, sliced

1 ½ cups (185 g/6 oz) finely grated Cheddar
1 cup (50 g/1⅔ oz) fresh basil leaves
½ cup (50 g/1¾ oz) grated fresh Parmesan

PREPARATION TIME 30 minutes
TOTAL COOKING TIME 1 hour 15 minutes
SERVES 6–8

1 Heat the oil in a large frying pan over medium heat. Cook the onion until soft. Add the garlic and cook for 1 minute. Add the tomato and simmer for 15 minutes. Season with salt. Preheat the oven to moderately hot 200°C (400°F/Gas 6).

2 Shallow-fry the eggplant in batches for 3–4 minutes, or until golden brown. Drain on paper towels.

3 Place one-third of the eggplant slices in a 1¾ litre ovenproof dish. Top with half the bocconcini and half the Cheddar. Repeat the layers, finishing with a layer of eggplant.

4 Pour over the tomato mixture. Scatter with torn basil leaves, then Parmesan. Bake for 40 minutes.

Variation

If you prefer not to fry the eggplant, brush it lightly with oil and brown lightly under a hot grill.

NUTRITION PER SERVE Protein 17 g; Fat 25 g; **Carbohydrate 7 g**; Dietary Fibre 5 g; Cholesterol 40 mg; 1340 kJ (320 cal)

Indonesian Vegetable and Coconut Curry

Curry paste
5 candlenuts
75 g (2½ oz) red Asian shallots
2 cloves garlic
2 teaspoons sambal oelek
¼ teaspoon ground turmeric
1 teaspoon grated fresh galangal
1 tablespoon peanut butter

2 tablespoons oil
1 onion, sliced

400 ml (13 fl oz) can coconut cream
200 g (6½ oz) carrots, julienned
200 g (6½ oz) snake beans, cut into 7 cm
(2¾ inch) lengths
300 g (10 oz) Chinese cabbage, roughly shredded
100 g (3½ oz) fresh shiitake mushrooms
¼ teaspoon sugar

PREPARATION TIME 20 minutes
TOTAL COOKING TIME 35 minutes
SERVES 6

1 To make the curry paste, place the candlenuts, red Asian shallots, garlic, sambal oelek, turmeric, galangal and peanut butter in a food processor, and process to a smooth paste.

2 Heat the oil in a large saucepan over low heat. Cook the curry paste, stirring, for 5 minutes, or until fragrant. Add the onion and cook for 5 minutes. Stir in ¼ cup (60 ml/2 fl oz) coconut cream and cook, stirring constantly, for 2 minutes, or until thickened. Add the carrot and snake beans, and cook over high heat for 3 minutes. Stir in the Chinese cabbage, mushrooms and 1 cup (250 ml/8 fl oz) water. Cook over high heat for 8–10 minutes, or until the vegetables are nearly cooked.

3 Stir in the remaining coconut cream and the sugar, and season to taste with salt. Bring to the boil, stirring constantly, then reduce the heat and simmer for 8–10 minutes to allow the flavours to develop. Serve hot.

NUTRITION PER SERVE Protein 5 g; Fat 22 g; **Carbohydrate 7.5 g**; Dietary Fibre 5 g; Cholesterol 0 mg; 1025 kJ (245 cal)

Prawn Curry

1 tablespoon butter
1 onion, finely chopped
1 clove garlic, crushed
1 1/2 tablespoons curry powder
2 tablespoons plain flour
2 cups (500 ml/16 fl oz) skim milk
1 kg (2 lb) raw prawns, peeled and deveined

1 1/2 tablespoons lemon juice
2 teaspoons sherry
1 tablespoon finely chopped fresh parsley

PREPARATION TIME 25 minutes
TOTAL COOKING TIME 15 minutes
SERVES 6

1 Heat the butter in a large saucepan. Add the onion and garlic, and cook for 5 minutes, or until softened. Add the curry powder and cook for 1 minute, then stir in the flour and cook for a further 1 minute.

2 Remove from the heat and stir in the milk until smooth. Return to the heat and stir constantly until the sauce has thickened.

3 Simmer for 2 minutes and then stir in the prawns. Continue to simmer for 5 minutes, or until the prawns are just cooked.

4 Stir in the lemon juice, sherry and parsley and serve immediately.

NUTRITION PER SERVE Protein 38 g; Fat 12 g; **Carbohydrate 9 g**; Dietary Fibre 1.5 g; Cholesterol 280 mg; 1247 kJ (298 cal)
NOTE Rice shown as a serving suggestion. Carbohydrate content not included in nutrition per serve.

Japanese Ginger Broth with Salmon

2 teaspoons dashi powder
3 x 3 cm (1 inch) pieces of fresh ginger, cut into
fine strips
8 spring onions, thinly sliced on the diagonal
750 g (1½ lb) baby bok choy, trimmed, leaves
separated
3 teaspoons Japanese soy sauce
200 g (6½ oz) soba noodles

2 tablespoons peanut oil
6 small salmon fillets, skin and bones removed
lime wedges, to serve

PREPARATION TIME 10 minutes
TOTAL COOKING TIME 15 minutes
SERVES 6

1 Place 1½ litres water and the dashi powder in a large saucepan. Bring to the boil and add the ginger, spring onion and bok choy. Reduce the heat and simmer, covered, for 5 minutes, or until the bok choy has wilted. Stir in the soy sauce, remove from the heat and keep warm.

2 Meanwhile, cook the noodles in a saucepan of boiling water for 1 minute, or until just tender. Drain and keep warm.

3 Heat the oil in a large frying pan, add the salmon fillets and cook for 3 minutes each side, or until cooked to your liking. (The salmon is best still rare in the middle.) Divide the noodles among six serving bowls. Add the bok choy and spoon on the broth. Top with the salmon fillets and serve with lime wedges.

NUTRITION PER SERVE Protein 21 g; Fat 20 g; **Carbohydrate 8 g**; Dietary Fibre 2.5 g; Cholesterol 0 mg; 1207 kJ (287 cal)

Fish Koftas in Tomato Curry Sauce

750 g (1 1/2 lb) firm fish fillets, such as snapper or
ling, roughly chopped
1 onion, chopped
2–3 cloves garlic, chopped
1 tablespoon grated fresh ginger
1/3 cup (20 g/3/4 oz) chopped fresh coriander leaves
1 teaspoon garam masala
1/4 teaspoon chilli powder
1 egg, lightly beaten
oil, for shallow-frying

Tomato curry sauce
2 tablespoons oil
1 large onion, finely chopped

3–4 cloves garlic, finely chopped
1 tablespoon grated fresh ginger
1 teaspoon ground turmeric
1 teaspoon ground cumin
1 teaspoon ground coriander
1/2 teaspoon garam masala
1/4 teaspoon chilli powder
2 x 400 g (13 oz) cans crushed tomatoes
1/4 cup (25 g/3/4 oz) chopped fresh coriander

PREPARATION TIME 40 minutes
TOTAL COOKING TIME 30 minutes
SERVES 6

1 Place the fish in a food processor and process until
smooth. Add the onion, garlic, ginger, coriander
leaves, garam masala, chilli powder and egg, and
process using the pulse button until well
combined. Using wetted hands, form 1 tablespoon
of the mixture into a ball. Repeat with the
remaining mixture.

2 To make the tomato curry sauce, heat the oil in a
large saucepan, add the onion, garlic and ginger,
and cook, stirring frequently, over medium heat for
8 minutes, or until lightly golden.

3 Add the spices and cook, stirring, for 2 minutes,
or until aromatic. Add the crushed tomato and
1 cup (250 ml/8 fl oz) water, then reduce the heat

and simmer, stirring frequently, for 15 minutes,
or until the sauce has reduced and thickened.

4 Meanwhile, heat 2 cm (3/4 inch) of the oil in a
large frying pan. Add the fish koftas in three to
four batches and cook for 3 minutes, or until
browned all over. Drain on paper towels.

5 Add the koftas to the sauce and simmer over low
heat for 5 minutes, or until heated through. Gently
fold in the coriander, season with salt and serve
with steamed rice and chapatis.

Note
The fish mixture is quite moist. Wetting your hands
will stop the mixture from sticking to them.

NUTRITION PER SERVE Protein 30 g; Fat 15 g; **Carbohydrate 7 g**; Dietary Fibre 3 g; Cholesterol 118 mg; 1145 kJ (273 cal)

Fish Fillets in Coconut Milk

2 long green chillies
2 small red chillies
2 stems lemon grass, white part only
2 coriander roots
4 kaffir lime leaves
2.1/2 cm (1 inch) piece fresh ginger, thinly sliced
2 cloves garlic, crushed
3 spring onions, finely sliced
1 teaspoon soft brown sugar
1 cup (250 ml/8 fl oz) coconut milk

400 g (13 oz) firm white fish fillets, cut into bite-sized pieces
1/2 cup (125 ml/4 fl oz) coconut cream
1 tablespoon fish sauce
2–3 tablespoons lime juice

PREPARATION TIME 10 minutes
TOTAL COOKING TIME 15 minutes
SERVES 4

1 Heat a wok until hot, then add the whole chillies and roast until just beginning to brown. Remove from the wok, cool and slice.

2 Bruise the lemon grass and coriander roots by crushing them with the flat side of a knife.

3 Add the lemon grass, coriander roots, kaffir lime leaves, ginger, garlic, spring onion, sugar and coconut milk to the wok. Stir and bring to the boil. Reduce the heat and simmer for 2 minutes. Add the fish pieces and simmer gently for 2–3 minutes or until the fish is tender. Stir in the coconut cream.

4 Stir through the chopped green and red chillies, fish sauce, salt and lime juice, to taste and serve immediately.

NUTRITION PER SERVE Protein 23 g; Fat 22 g; **Carbohydrate 6.5 g**; Dietary Fibre 2.5 g; Cholesterol 70 mg; 1323 kJ (316 cal)

Seafood Casserole with Feta and Olives

500 g (1 lb) fresh mussels
2 tablespoons olive oil
1 large onion, sliced
2 x 400 g (13 oz) cans tomatoes, chopped
2 strips lemon rind
1 tablespoon chopped fresh lemon thyme
1/3 cup (80 ml/2¾ fl oz) dry vermouth or white wine
1 teaspoon sugar
12 raw king prawns, peeled and deveined,
tails intact

750 g (1½ lb) firm white fish fillets, cut into bite-size pieces
12 black olives
125 g (4 oz) feta cheese, cubed

PREPARATION TIME 20 minutes
TOTAL COOKING TIME 35 minutes
SERVES 4

1 Discard any open mussels. Scrub the rest of the mussels and remove the beards. Place the mussels in a saucepan of simmering water. As soon as the shells open, place the mussels in a bowl of cold water, discarding any unopened ones. Open them up and leave on their half shells, discarding the other half.

2 Preheat the oven to moderate 180°C (350°F/Gas 4). Heat the oil in a large, heavy-based saucepan and cook the onion over low heat for 5 minutes, or until soft but not brown. Add the tomato, lemon rind, lemon thyme, vermouth and sugar. Bring to the boil, and season to taste. Reduce the heat, cover and simmer for 10 minutes.

3 Place the seafood in a shallow ovenproof dish and cover with the hot sauce. Bake, covered, for 10 minutes. Add the olives and feta, covering the seafood with the sauce. Bake for 10 minutes, or until heated through. Serve immediately.

NUTRITION PER SERVE Protein 70 g; Fat 25 g; **Carbohydrate 10 g**; Dietary Fibre 4 g; Cholesterol 313 mg; 2430 kJ (580 cal)

Chicken San Choy Bau

1 tablespoon oil
750 g (1½ lb) chicken mince
2 cloves garlic, finely chopped
100 g (3½ oz) can water chestnuts, drained and chopped
1½ tablespoons oyster sauce
3 teaspoons soy sauce

1 teaspoon sugar
5 spring onions, finely sliced
4 iceberg lettuce leaves

PREPARATION TIME 10 minutes
TOTAL COOKING TIME 5 minutes
SERVES 4 as a light lunch

1 Heat a wok or frying pan over high heat, add the oil and swirl to coat. Add the chicken mince and garlic and stir-fry for 3–4 minutes, or until browned and cooked through, breaking up any lumps with the back of a spoon. Pour off any excess liquid.

2 Reduce the heat and add the water chestnuts, oyster sauce, soy sauce, sugar and spring onion.

3 Trim the lettuce leaves around the edges to neaten them and to form a cup shape. Divide the chicken mixture among the lettuce cups and serve hot, with extra oyster sauce.

Variation
Drizzle some hoisin sauce over the top before serving.

NUTRITION PER SERVE Protein 40 g; Fat 9 g; **Carbohydrate 6 g**; Dietary Fibre 2 g; Cholesterol 88 mg; 1142 kJ (273 cal)

Lime Steamed Chicken

2 limes, thinly sliced
4 chicken breast fillets
1 bunch (500 g/1 lb) bok choy
1 bunch (500 g/1 lb) choy sum
1 teaspoon sesame oil
1 tablespoon peanut oil

½ cup (125 ml/4 fl oz) oyster sauce
⅓ cup (80 ml/2¾ fl oz) lime juice

PREPARATION TIME 15 minutes
TOTAL COOKING TIME 15 minutes
SERVES 4

1 Line the base of a bamboo steamer with the lime, place the chicken on top and season. Place over a wok with a little water in the base, cover and steam for 8–10 minutes, or until the chicken is cooked through. Cover the chicken and keep warm. Remove the water from the wok.

2 Wash and trim the greens. Heat the oils in the wok and cook the greens for 2–3 minutes, or until just wilted.

3 Combine the oyster sauce and lime juice and pour over the greens when they are cooked. Place the chicken on serving plates on top of the greens and serve with rice and lime slices.

Note
The Asian green vegetables used in this recipe, bok choy and choy sum, can be replaced by any green vegetables, such as broccoli, snow peas, or English spinach.

NUTRITION PER SERVE Protein 60 g; Fat 12 g; **Carbohydrate 10 g**; Dietary Fibre 4.5 g; Cholesterol 120 mg; 1665 kJ (398 cal)

Peppered Chicken Stir-fry

1 tablespoon oil
2 chicken breast fillets, cut into strips
2$\frac{1}{2}$ teaspoons seasoned peppercorns (see NOTE)
1 onion, cut into wedges
1 red capsicum, cut into strips
2 tablespoons oyster sauce

1 teaspoon soy sauce
1 teaspoon sugar

PREPARATION TIME 10 minutes
TOTAL COOKING TIME 10 minutes
SERVES 4

1 Heat a wok or frying pan over high heat, add the oil and swirl to coat. Add the chicken strips and stir-fry for 2–3 minutes, or until browned.

2 Add the peppercorns and stir-fry until fragrant. Add the onion and capsicum and stir-fry for 2 minutes, or until the vegetables have just softened slightly.

3 Reduce the heat and stir in the oyster sauce, soy and sugar. Serve hot.

Note
Seasoned peppercorns are available in the herb and spice section of supermarkets.

NUTRITION PER SERVE Protein 18 g; Fat 6.5 g; **Carbohydrate 6 g**; Dietary Fibre 1 g; Cholesterol 40 mg; 665 kJ (160 cal)

Chicken Chasseur

1 kg (2 lb) chicken thigh fillets
1 tablespoon oil
1 clove garlic, crushed
1 large onion, sliced
100 g (3½ oz) button mushrooms, sliced
1 teaspoon thyme leaves

400 g (13 oz) can chopped tomatoes
¼ cup (60 ml/2 fl oz) chicken stock
¼ cup (60 ml/2 fl oz) white wine
1 tablespoon tomato paste

PREPARATION TIME 20 minutes
TOTAL COOKING TIME 1 hour 30 minutes
SERVES 4

1 Preheat the oven to moderate 180°C (350°F/Gas 4). Trim the chicken of any fat and sinew. Heat the oil in a heavy-based frying pan and brown the chicken in batches over medium heat. Drain on paper towels and then transfer to a casserole dish.

2 Add the garlic, onion and mushrooms to the pan and cook over medium heat for 5 minutes, or until soft. Add to the chicken with the thyme and tomatoes.

3 Combine the stock, wine and tomato paste and pour over the chicken. Cover and bake for 1¼ hours, or until the chicken is tender and cooked through.

Storage time
Best cooked a day in advance to let the flavours develop.

NUTRITION PER SERVE Protein 60 g; Fat 12 g; **Carbohydrate 6 g**; Dietary Fibre 2 g; Cholesterol 125 mg; 1710 kJ (410 cal)

Chicken Curry with Apricots

18 dried apricots
1 tablespoon ghee or oil
2 x 1½ kg (3 lb) chickens, jointed
3 onions, thinly sliced
1 teaspoon grated fresh ginger
3 cloves garlic, crushed
3 large fresh green chillies, seeded and finely chopped
1 teaspoon cumin seeds

1 teaspoon chilli powder
½ teaspoon ground turmeric
4 cardamom pods, bruised
4 large tomatoes, peeled and cut into eighths

PREPARATION TIME 40 minutes + 1 hour soaking
TOTAL COOKING TIME 1 hour 10 minutes
SERVES 6–8

1 Soak the dried apricots in 1 cup (250 ml/8 fl oz) hot water for 1 hour.

2 Melt the ghee in a large saucepan, add the chicken in batches and cook over high heat for 5–6 minutes, or until browned. Remove from the pan. Add the onion and cook, stirring often, for 10 minutes, or until the onion has softened and turned golden brown.

3 Add the ginger, garlic and chopped green chilli, and cook, stirring, for 2 minutes. Stir in the cumin seeds, chilli powder and ground turmeric, and cook for a further 1 minute.

4 Return the chicken to the pan, add the cardamom, tomato and apricots, with any remaining liquid, and mix well. Simmer, covered, for 35 minutes, or until the chicken is tender.

5 Remove the chicken, cover and keep warm. Bring the liquid to the boil and boil rapidly, uncovered, for 5 minutes, or until it has thickened slightly. To serve, spoon the liquid over the chicken. Serve with steamed rice mixed with raisins, grated carrot and toasted flaked almonds.

NUTRITION PER SERVE Protein 44 g; Fat 6.5 g; **Carbohydrate 6.5 g**; Dietary Fibre 2.5 g; Cholesterol 100 mg; 1105 kJ (264 cal) NOTE Rice shown as a serving suggestion. Carbohydrate content not included in nutrition per serve.

Chicken Meatballs

500 g (1 lb) chicken mince
3 tablespoons fresh breadcrumbs
2 teaspoons finely chopped fresh thyme
1 tablespoon oil
1 onion, finely chopped
2 x 425 g (14 oz) cans diced tomatoes
2 teaspoons balsamic vinegar

1 cup (250 ml/8 fl oz) chicken stock
grated Parmesan, to serve

PREPARATION TIME 15 minutes
TOTAL COOKING TIME 30 minutes
SERVES 6

1 Combine the chicken mince, breadcrumbs and thyme in a large bowl and season well. Roll tablespoons of the mixture between your hands to make meatballs.

2 Heat the oil in a large non-stick frying pan and cook the meatballs in batches for 5–8 minutes, or until golden brown. Remove from the pan and drain well on paper towels.

3 Add the onion to the pan and cook for 2–3 minutes, or until softened. Add the tomato, vinegar and stock, return the meatballs to the pan, then reduce the heat and simmer for 10 minutes, or until the sauce thickens and the meatballs are cooked through.

NUTRITION PER SERVE Protein 20 g; Fat 8.5 g; **Carbohydrate 7.5 g**; Dietary Fibre 2 g; Cholesterol 42 mg; 812 kJ (194 cal)

Pork with Snake Beans

1 tablespoon oil
400 g (13 oz) pork fillet, cut into thick slices
2 onions, thinly sliced
150 g (5 oz) snake beans, diagonally sliced
(see NOTE)
3 cloves garlic, finely chopped
1 tablespoon finely chopped fresh ginger

1 red capsicum, thinly sliced
6 spring onions, diagonally sliced
2 tablespoons sweet chilli sauce

PREPARATION TIME 15 minutes
TOTAL COOKING TIME 20 minutes
SERVES 4

1 Heat the wok until very hot, add half the oil and swirl it around to coat the side of the wok. Stir-fry the pork in two batches over high heat for 3–4 minutes, or until it is just cooked, adding a little more oil if necessary for the second batch. Remove all the pork from the wok.

2 Heat the remaining oil in the wok over medium heat and add the sliced onion. Cook for 3–4 minutes, or until the onion has softened slightly. Add the sliced snake beans and cook for 2–3 minutes. Add the garlic, ginger, capsicum and spring onion, and toss well. Increase the heat and cook for 3–4 minutes.

3 Return the pork to the wok, add the sweet chilli sauce and toss well. Remove from the heat and season with salt and pepper. Serve immediately.

Note
If you can't find snake beans you can use ordinary green beans in this recipe.

NUTRITION PER SERVE Protein 25 g; Fat 12 g; **Carbohydrate 8 g**; Dietary Fibre 4 g; Cholesterol 50 mg; 1005 kJ (240 cal)

Barbecued Pork and Broccoli Stir-fry

1 tablespoon oil
1 large onion, thinly sliced
2 carrots, cut into matchsticks
200 g (6$\frac{1}{2}$ oz) broccoli, cut into bite-sized florets
6 spring onions, diagonally sliced
1 tablespoon finely chopped fresh ginger
3 cloves garlic, finely chopped
400 g (13 oz) Chinese barbecued pork, thinly sliced (see NOTE)

2 tablespoons soy sauce
2 tablespoons mirin
2 cups (180 g/6 oz) bean sprouts

PREPARATION TIME 25 minutes
TOTAL COOKING TIME 10 minutes
SERVES 4–6

1 Heat the wok until very hot, add the oil and swirl it around to coat the side. Stir-fry the onion over medium heat for 3–4 minutes, or until slightly softened. Add the carrot, broccoli, spring onion, ginger and garlic, and stir-fry for 4–5 minutes.

2 Increase the heat to high and add the barbecued pork. Toss constantly until the pork is well mixed with the vegetables and is heated through. Add the soy sauce and mirin, and toss until the ingredients are well coated. (The wok should be hot enough that the sauce reduces a little to form a glaze-like consistency.) Add the bean sprouts and season well with salt and pepper. Serve immediately.

Note
Chinese barbecued pork is available from Asian barbecue shops.

NUTRITION PER SERVE Protein 20 g; Fat 15 g; **Carbohydrate 6.5 g**; Dietary Fibre 6 g; Cholesterol 40 mg; 920 kJ (220 cal)

Pork and Eggplant Hotpot

olive oil, for cooking
375 g (12 oz) slender eggplant, cut into 3 cm
(1 ¼ inch) slices
8 bulb spring onions
400 g (13 oz) can chopped tomatoes
2 cloves garlic, crushed
2 teaspoons ground cumin
500 g (1 lb) pork fillet, cut into 3 cm (1 ¼ inch)
thick slices

seasoned plain flour
⅔ cup (170 ml/5½ fl oz) cider
1 sprig fresh rosemary
2 tablespoons finely chopped toasted almonds

PREPARATION TIME 20 minutes
TOTAL COOKING TIME 1 hour 40 minutes
SERVES 4

1 Heat ¼ cup (60 ml/2 fl oz) of oil in a large, heavy-based frying pan. Brown the eggplant in batches over high heat, adding oil as needed. Remove and set aside.

2 Quarter the spring onions along their length. Add some oil to the pan and fry the spring onion over medium heat for 5 minutes. Add the tomato, garlic and cumin, and cook for 2 minutes. Remove and set aside.

3 Coat the pork in the seasoned flour, shaking off any excess. Brown in batches over medium–high heat until golden, adding oil as needed. Remove and set aside.

4 Add the cider to the pan and stir well, scraping down the side and base. Allow to boil for 1–2 minutes, then add ½ cup (125 ml/4 fl oz) water. Reduce the heat and stir in the spring onion and tomato. Add the pork, season, and poke the rosemary sprig into the stew. Partially cover and simmer gently for 20 minutes.

5 Layer the eggplant on top, partially cover and cook for 25 minutes, or until the pork is tender. Just before serving, gently toss the almonds through.

NUTRITION PER SERVE Protein 30 g; Fat 7 g; **Carbohydrate 10 g**; Dietary Fibre 5 g; Cholesterol 60 mg; 980 kJ (235 cal)

Pork and Tamarind Curry

⅓ cup (80 ml/2¾ fl oz) oil
2 onions, thickly sliced
4 large cloves garlic, crushed
3 tablespoons Sri Lankan curry powder
1 tablespoon grated fresh ginger
10 dried curry leaves or 5 fresh curry leaves
2 teaspoons chilli powder
¼ teaspoon fenugreek seeds
1¼ kg (2 lb 8 oz) lean shoulder pork, cubed
1 stem lemon grass (white part only), finely chopped
2 tablespoons tamarind purée
4 cardamom pods, crushed
400 ml (13 fl oz) can coconut cream

Cucumber sambal

1–2 large cucumbers, halved, seeded and finely chopped
2 cups (500 g/16 oz) plain yoghurt
2 tablespoons fresh coriander leaves, finely chopped
1 tablespoon lemon juice
2 cloves garlic, crushed

PREPARATION TIME 20 minutes
TOTAL COOKING TIME 1 hour 50 minutes
SERVES 6

1 Heat the oil in a heavy-based Dutch oven or deep, lidded frying pan. Add the onion, garlic, curry powder, ginger, curry leaves, chilli powder, fenugreek and 1 teaspoon salt, and cook, stirring, over medium heat for 5 minutes.

2 Add the pork, lemon grass, tamarind purée, cardamom and 1½ cups (375 ml/12 fl oz) hot water, then reduce the heat and simmer, covered, for 1 hour.

3 Stir in the coconut cream and simmer, uncovered, for 40–45 minutes, or until the sauce has reduced and become thick and creamy.

4 To make the cucumber sambal, place the cucumber in a bowl and stir in the yoghurt, coriander, lemon juice and garlic. Season to taste.

5 Serve the curry with the cucumber sambal.

NUTRITION PER SERVE Protein 55 g; Fat 30 g; **Carbohydrate 9.5 g**; Dietary Fibre 3 g; Cholesterol 110 mg; 2260 kJ (540 cal)

Peppered Lamb and Asparagus Stir-fry

400 g (13 oz) lamb fillets
2 teaspoons green peppercorns, finely chopped
3 cloves garlic, finely chopped
1 tablespoon oil
1 onion, cut into small wedges
$1/3$ cup (80 ml/$2^3/4$ fl oz) dry sherry
1 green capsicum, cut into strips
$1/2$ teaspoon sugar
16 small asparagus spears, cut into bite-sized pieces, tough ends discarded

200 g ($6^1/2$ oz) broccoli florets
2 tablespoons oyster sauce
garlic chives, cut into short lengths, to garnish

PREPARATION TIME 35 minutes + 20 minutes marinating
TOTAL COOKING TIME 20 minutes
SERVES 4

1 Trim away any sinew from the lamb and cut the lamb into bite-sized pieces. Combine in a bowl with the green peppercorns, garlic and oil, then toss well and set aside for 20 minutes.

2 Heat a wok over high heat until slightly smoking. Add the pieces of lamb and stir-fry in batches until brown and just cooked. Remove, cover and keep warm.

3 Reheat the wok and stir-fry the onion and 2 teaspoons of the sherry for 1 minute. Add the capsicum, sugar and a large pinch of salt. Cover, steam for 2 minutes, add the asparagus, broccoli, then remaining sherry, and stir-fry for 1 minute. Cover and steam for 3 minutes, or until the vegetables are just tender. Return the lamb to the pan, add the oyster sauce and stir to combine with the vegetables. Serve garnished with the chives.

NUTRITION PER SERVE Protein 25 g; Fat 12 g; **Carbohydrate 8 g**; Dietary Fibre 4 g; Cholesterol 65 mg; 1100 kJ (265 cal)

PRETTY GOOD

Lamb Kefta

1 kg (2 lb) lamb mince
1 onion, finely chopped
2 cloves garlic, finely chopped
2 tablespoons finely chopped fresh flat-leaf parsley
2 tablespoons finely chopped fresh coriander leaves
$\frac{1}{2}$ teaspoon cayenne pepper
$\frac{1}{2}$ teaspoon ground allspice
$\frac{1}{2}$ teaspoon ground ginger
$\frac{1}{2}$ teaspoon ground cardamom
1 teaspoon ground cumin
1 teaspoon paprika

Sauce
2 tablespoons olive oil
1 onion, finely chopped
2 cloves garlic, finely chopped
2 teaspoons ground cumin
$\frac{1}{2}$ teaspoon ground cinnamon
1 teaspoon paprika
2 x 425 g (14 oz) cans chopped tomatoes
2 teaspoons harissa
$\frac{1}{3}$ cup (20 g/$\frac{3}{4}$ oz) chopped fresh coriander leaves

PREPARATION TIME 30 minutes
TOTAL COOKING TIME 40 minutes
SERVES 4

1 Preheat the oven to moderate 180°C (350°F/Gas 4). Lightly grease two baking trays. Place the lamb, onion, garlic, herbs and spices in a bowl, and mix together well. Season with salt and pepper. Roll tablespoons of the mixture into balls and place on the trays. Bake for 18–20 minutes, or until browned.

2 Meanwhile, to make the sauce, heat the oil in a large saucepan, add the onion and cook over medium heat for 5 minutes, or until soft. Add the garlic, cumin, cinnamon and paprika, and cook for 1 minute, or until fragrant.

3 Stir in the tomato and harissa, and bring to the boil. Reduce the heat and simmer for 20 minutes, then add the meatballs and simmer for 10 minutes, or until cooked through. Stir in the coriander, season well, and serve.

NUTRITION PER SERVE Protein 53 g; Fat 37 g; **Carbohydrate 10 g**; Dietary Fibre 4 g; Cholesterol 158 mg; 2434 kJ (580 cal)

Creamy Veal and Mushroom Stew

750 g (1 ¹/₂ lb) veal steaks, cut into 1 cm (¹/₂ inch)
strips
¹/₄ cup (30 g/1 oz) plain flour
30 g (1 oz) butter
1 clove garlic, crushed
1 tablespoon Dijon mustard
1 cup (250 ml/8 fl oz) cream
¹/₂ cup (125 ml/4 fl oz) white wine

1 tablespoon chopped fresh thyme
1 cup (250 ml/8 fl oz) chicken stock
375 g (12 oz) button mushrooms, halved

PREPARATION TIME 20 minutes
TOTAL COOKING TIME 2 hours
SERVES 4

1 Toss the meat in the flour, shaking off the excess. Heat the butter and garlic in a heavy-based saucepan. Add the meat and cook quickly in small batches over medium heat until well browned. Drain on paper towels.

2 Return the meat to the pan and add the mustard, cream, wine, thyme and stock. Bring to the boil, then reduce the heat and simmer, covered, for 1¹/₂ hours, stirring occasionally.

3 Add the mushrooms and cook for a further 15 minutes, or until the meat is tender.

NUTRITION PER SERVE Protein 47 g; Fat 38 g; **Carbohydrate 8.5 g**; Dietary Fibre 3 g; Cholesterol 258 mg; 2425 kJ (580 cal)

Beef Teriyaki with Cucumber Salad

4 scotch fillet steaks
80 ml (⅓ cup) soy sauce
2 tablespoons mirin
1 tablespoon sake (optional)
1 clove garlic, crushed
1 teaspoon grated fresh ginger
1 teaspoon sugar
1 teaspoon toasted sesame seeds

Cucumber salad
1 large Lebanese cucumber, peeled,
seeded and diced
½ red capsicum, diced
2 spring onions, sliced thinly on the diagonal
2 teaspoons sugar
1 tablespoon rice vinegar

PREPARATION TIME 20 minutes + 30 minutes refrigeration + 10 minutes resting
TOTAL COOKING TIME 20 minutes
SERVES 4

1 Place the steaks in a non-metallic dish. Combine the soy, mirin, sake, garlic and ginger and pour over the steaks. Cover with plastic wrap and refrigerate for at least 30 minutes.

2 To make the cucumber salad, place the cucumber, capsicum and spring onion in a small bowl. Place the sugar, rice vinegar and 60 ml (¼ cup) water in a small saucepan and stir over medium heat until the sugar dissolves. Increase the heat and simmer rapidly for 3–4 minutes, or until slightly thickened. Pour over the cucumber salad, stir to combine and leave to cool completely.

3 Spray a chargrill or hot plate with oil spray and heat until very hot. Drain the steaks and reserve the marinade. Cook for 3–4 minutes on each side, or until cooked to your liking. Remove and rest the meat for 5–10 minutes before slicing.

4 Meanwhile, place the sugar and the reserved marinade in a small saucepan and heat, stirring, until the sugar has dissolved. Bring to the boil, then simmer for 2–3 minutes, remove from the heat and keep warm.

5 Slice each steak into 1 cm (½ inch) strips, being careful to keep the steak in its shape. Arrange the steak on each plate. Spoon on some of the marinade, a spoonful of cucumber salad and garnish with sesame seeds. Serve with the remaining cucumber salad.

NUTRITION PER SERVE Protein 23 g; Fat 5 g; **Carbohydrate 6 g**; Dietary Fibre 1 g; Cholesterol 67 mg; 720 kJ (170 Cal)

Beef with Oyster Sauce

1 1/2 teaspoons cornflour
1/2 cup (125 ml/4 fl oz) beef stock
2 tablespoons oyster sauce
1 teaspoon finely crushed garlic
1 teaspoon caster sugar
1 tablespoon oil
350 g (11 oz) rump steak, finely sliced
250 g (8 oz) beans, topped and tailed, cut into 5 cm (2 inch) lengths

1 small red capsicum, sliced
1/2 cup (60 g/2 oz) bean sprouts

PREPARATION TIME 15 minutes
TOTAL COOKING TIME 5 minutes
SERVES 4

1 Dissolve the cornflour in a little of the stock. Mix with the remaining stock, oyster sauce, garlic and sugar and set aside.

2 Heat the wok until very hot, add the oil and swirl it around to coat the side. Add the beef in batches and stir-fry over high heat for 2 minutes, or until it browns.

3 Add the beans and capsicum and stir-fry for another minute.

4 Add the cornflour mixture to the wok and cook until the sauce boils and thickens. Stir in the bean sprouts and serve immediately.

NUTRITION PER SERVE Protein 23 g; Fat 12 g; **Carbohydrate 10 g**; Dietary Fibre 2.5 g; Cholesterol 60 mg; 1016 kJ (243 cal)

Spiced Beef

⅓ cup (60 g/2 oz) soft brown sugar
1 teaspoon ground cinnamon
1 teaspoon ground nutmeg
1 teaspoon ground cardamom
1 teaspoon ground black pepper
1½ kg (3 lb) piece fresh silverside, trimmed
1 orange, quartered

1 large onion, quartered
¼ cup (60 ml/2 fl oz) red wine vinegar

PREPARATION TIME 20 minutes
TOTAL COOKING TIME 1 hour 40 minutes
SERVES 4–6

1 Preheat the oven to warm 160°C (315°F/Gas 2–3). Combine the sugar, cinnamon, nutmeg, cardamom and pepper in a small bowl. Rub the mixture all over the meat, pressing it on firmly with your fingers. Place the meat in a deep casserole dish.

2 Place the orange and onion around the meat, and pour in the vinegar combined with 1 cup (250 ml/8 fl oz) water. Bake, covered, for 1–1½ hours, or until the meat is tender.

3 Remove the meat from the dish, cover and set aside. Remove the orange pieces from the cooking liquid. Strain the remaining cooking liquid into a shallow saucepan and cook, uncovered, for 10 minutes, or until reduced by half. Serve the meat warm or cold, accompanied by the sauce.

Note
To serve the silverside cold, refrigerate it overnight in the cooking liquid before draining.

A whole piece of rump or topside steak may be used in place of the fresh silverside.

NUTRITION PER SERVE Protein 56 g; Fat 5.5 g; **Carbohydrate 10 g**; Dietary Fibre 0.5 g; Cholesterol 168 mg; 1325 kJ (315 cal)

Red Beef and Eggplant Curry

1 cup (250 ml/8 fl oz) coconut cream (do not shake the can)
2 tablespoons red curry paste
500 g (1 lb) round or topside steak, cut into strips (see NOTE)
2 tablespoons fish sauce
1 tablespoon palm sugar or soft brown sugar
5 kaffir lime leaves, halved

2 cups (500 ml/16 fl oz) coconut milk
8 Thai eggplants, halved
2 tablespoons finely shredded fresh Thai basil leaves

PREPARATION TIME 40 minutes
TOTAL COOKING TIME 1 hour 30 minutes
SERVES 4

1 Place the thick coconut cream from the top of the can in a wok and bring to the boil. Boil for 10 minutes, or until the oil starts to separate. Add the curry paste and simmer, stirring to prevent it sticking to the bottom, for 5 minutes, or until fragrant.

2 Add the meat and cook, stirring, for 3–5 minutes, or until it changes colour. Add the fish sauce, palm sugar, lime leaves, coconut milk and remaining coconut cream, and simmer for 1 hour, or until the meat is tender and the sauce has slightly thickened.

3 Add the eggplant and cook for 10 minutes, or until tender. If the sauce is too thick, add a little water. Stir in half the shredded basil leaves. Garnish with the remaining basil leaves.

Note
Cut the meat into 5 x 5 x 2 cm (2 x 2 x ¾ inch) pieces, then cut across the grain at a 45° angle into ½ cm (¼ inch) thick slices.

NUTRITION PER SERVE Protein 30 g; Fat 43 g; **Carbohydrate 10 g**; Dietary Fibre 5 g; Cholesterol 85 mg; 2276 kJ (544 cal)

Beef and Red Wine Stew

30 g (1 oz) butter
2 tablespoons oil
1 kg (2 lb) topside steak, trimmed and cut into
3 cm (1 $\frac{1}{4}$ inch) cubes
100 g (3 $\frac{1}{2}$ oz) bacon pieces, cut into 1 $\frac{1}{2}$ cm
($\frac{5}{8}$ inch) cubes
18 baby onions
2 cloves garlic, crushed

$\frac{1}{4}$ cup (30 g/1 oz) plain flour
2 cups (500 ml/16 fl oz) red wine
3 cups (750 ml/24 fl oz) beef stock
300 g (10 oz) small mushrooms, halved

PREPARATION TIME 15 minutes
TOTAL COOKING TIME 2 hours
SERVES 6

1 Heat the butter and oil in a heavy-based saucepan. Cook the meat quickly in small batches over medium–high heat until browned, then drain on paper towels.

2 Add the bacon, onions and garlic to the pan, and cook, stirring, for 2 minutes, or until browned. Add the flour and stir over low heat until lightly golden. Gradually pour in the wine and stock, and stir until smooth. Stir continuously over medium heat for 2 minutes, or until the mixture boils and thickens.

3 Return the meat to the pan and reduce the heat to a simmer. Cook, covered, for 1 $\frac{1}{2}$ hours, or until the meat is tender, stirring occasionally. Add the mushrooms and cook for 15 minutes.

NUTRITION PER SERVE Protein 45 g; Fat 17 g; **Carbohydrate 10 g**; Dietary Fibre 2.5 g; Cholesterol 105 mg; 1800 kJ (430 cal)

Raspberry Mousse

3 teaspoons gelatine
1 cup (250 g/8 oz) low-fat vanilla yoghurt
2 x 200 g (6½ oz) tubs low-fat fromage frais or
light vanilla Fruche
4 egg whites
150 g (5 oz) raspberries, mashed
fresh raspberries and mint leaves, for serving

PREPARATION TIME 30 minutes + refrigeration
SERVES 4

1 Sprinkle the gelatine in an even layer onto
1 tablespoon water in a small bowl and leave to
go spongy. Bring a small pan of water to the boil,
remove from the heat and place the bowl in the
pan. Stir until clear.

2 In a large bowl, stir the vanilla yoghurt and
fromage frais together, then add the gelatine and
mix well.

3 Using electric beaters, beat the egg whites until
stiff peaks form, then fold through the yoghurt
mixture. Transfer half to a separate bowl and fold
the mashed raspberries through.

4 Divide the raspberry mixture into the bases of
4 long glasses or serving bowls. Top with the vanilla
mixture. Refrigerate for several hours, or until set.
Decorate with fresh raspberries and mint leaves.

NUTRITION PER SERVE Protein 9.5 g; Fat 2 g; **Carbohydrate 10 g**; Dietary Fibre 2 g; Cholesterol 4 mg; 355 kJ (85 cal)

Individual Lemon and Passionfruit Tarts with Raspberries

60 g (2½ oz) low-fat margarine
90 g (⅓ cup) caster (superfine) sugar
2 eggs
2 tablespoons self-raising flour, sifted
60 ml (¼ cup) lemon juice
1 teaspoon grated lemon zest
1 passionfruit, pulp removed

3 sheets filo pastry
125 g (4½ oz) fresh raspberries

PREPARATION TIME 15 minutes
TOTAL COOKING TIME 25 minutes
MAKES 6

1 Preheat the oven to 180°C (350°F/Gas 4). Beat the margarine and sugar until light and creamy. Add the eggs one at a time, beating well after each addition.

2 Add the flour, lemon juice, zest and passionfruit pulp and beat until well combined.

3 Fold each sheet of filo pastry in half from the short end up. Fold again and cut in half. Carefully line six 125 ml (½ cup) muffin holes with a piece of pastry. Pour in the lemon mixture and bake for 20–25 minutes, or until set. Serve topped with the fresh raspberries and, if desired, whipped light cream.

NUTRITION PER TART Fat 6 g; Protein 3.5 g; **Carbohydrate 9 g**; Dietary Fibre 2 g; Cholesterol 60 mg; 435 kJ (105 Cal)

Passionfruit Bavarois

2 x 170 g (5½ oz) cans passionfruit in syrup
300 g (10 oz) silken tofu, chopped
600 ml (20 fl oz) buttermilk
2 tablespoons caster sugar
1 teaspoon vanilla essence
6 teaspoons gelatine

¾ cup (185 ml/6 fl oz) passionfruit pulp

PREPARATION TIME 10 minutes + overnight refrigeration
SERVES 8

1 Push the passionfruit in syrup through a sieve. Discard the seeds. Combine the strained syrup with the tofu, buttermilk, caster sugar and vanilla in a blender. Blend for 90 seconds on high, to mix thoroughly. Leave in the blender.

2 Put ⅓ cup (80 ml/2¾ fl oz) water in a small bowl and put the bowl in a slightly larger bowl of boiling water. Sprinkle the gelatine onto the water in the small bowl and stir until dissolved. Leave to cool.

3 Place eight 200 ml (6½ fl oz) dariole moulds in a baking dish. Add the gelatine to the blender and mix on high for 1 minute. Pour into the moulds, cover the dish with plastic wrap and refrigerate overnight.

4 When ready to serve, carefully run a spatula around the edge of each mould and dip the bases into hot water for 2 seconds to make removal easier. Place each on a plate and spoon the passionfruit pulp around the bases. Serve, topped with a few halved strawberries.

NUTRITION PER SERVE Protein 8 g; Fat 2.5 g; **Carbohydrate 10 g**; Dietary Fibre 10 g; Cholesterol 3 mg; 455 kJ (110 cal)

Coeur à la Crème with Berries

100 g (3½ oz) low-fat ricotta cheese
65 g (2½ oz) fat-reduced cream cheese
65 g (2½ oz) light sour cream
2 tablespoons icing (confectioners') sugar
1 egg white
170 g (6 oz) mixed berries (strawberries,
blueberries, raspberries)
icing (confectioners') sugar, extra, to dust

PREPARATION TIME 20 minutes + overnight
refrigeration
SERVES 4

1 Beat the ricotta, cream cheese and sour cream with 1 tablespoon icing sugar until mixed. Beat the egg white in a separate clean bowl until stiff peaks form, then carefully fold into cheese mixture with a metal spoon.

2 Line four ceramic heart-shaped moulds with a square of dampened muslin. Fill with the cheese mixture. Bring the remaining muslin up over the top to cover and lightly press. Put the moulds on a tray and refrigerate for 6 hours, or preferably overnight.

3 Blend half the berries and the remaining sugar in a food processor until combined. Strain.

4 To serve, unmould the crèmes onto a plate and place a pile of berries to the side. Drizzle with the purée and dust with icing sugar.

NUTRITION PER SERVE Fat 8 g; Protein 6 g; **Carbohydrate 10 g**; Dietary Fibre 1.5 g; Cholesterol 29 mg; 570 kJ (135 Cal)

Brazil Nut and Coffee Biscotti

3 teaspoons instant coffee powder
1 tablespoon dark rum, warmed
2 eggs
$\frac{1}{2}$ cup (125 g/4 oz) caster sugar
$1\frac{1}{4}$ cups (155 g/5 oz) plain flour
$\frac{1}{2}$ cup (60 g/2 oz) self-raising flour
1 teaspoon ground cinnamon

$\frac{3}{4}$ cup (105 g/3$\frac{1}{2}$ oz) brazil nuts, roughly chopped
1 tablespoon caster sugar, extra

PREPARATION TIME 20 minutes
TOTAL COOKING TIME 45 minutes
MAKES 40 pieces

1 Preheat the oven to 180°C (350°F/Gas 4). Dissolve the coffee in the rum. Beat the eggs and sugar until thick and creamy, then beat in the coffee. Sift the flours and cinnamon into a bowl, then stir in the nuts. Mix in the egg mixture.

2 Divide the mixture into two rolls, each about 28 cm (11 inches) long. Line a baking tray with baking paper, put the rolls on it and press lightly to flatten to about 6 cm (2$\frac{1}{2}$ inches) across. Brush lightly with water and sprinkle with the extra sugar. Bake for 25 minutes, or until firm and light brown. Cool until warm on the tray. Reduce the oven temperature to warm 160°C (315°F/Gas 2–3).

3 Cut into 1 cm ($\frac{1}{2}$ inch) thick diagonal slices. Bake in a single layer on the lined tray for 20 minutes, or until dry, turning once. Cool on a rack. When cold, store in an airtight container for 2–3 weeks.

NUTRITION PER BISCOTTI Protein 1 g; Fat 1.5 g; **Carbohydrate 7.5 g**; Dietary Fibre 0 g; Cholesterol 9 mg; 210 kJ (50 cal)

Pesto Beef Salad

100 g (3½ oz) button mushrooms
1 large yellow capsicum
1 large red capsicum
cooking oil spray
100 g (3½ oz) lean fillet steak
1½ cups (135 g/4½ oz) penne

Pesto
1 cup (50 g/1¾ oz) tightly packed basil leaves
2 cloves garlic, chopped
2 tablespoons pepitas (pumpkin seeds)
1 tablespoon olive oil
2 tablespoons orange juice
1 tablespoon lemon juice

PREPARATION TIME 30 minutes
TOTAL COOKING TIME 25 minutes
SERVES 8 as a starter

1 Cut the mushrooms into quarters. Cut the capsicums into large flat pieces, removing the seeds and membrane. Place skin-side-up under a hot grill until blackened. Leave covered with a tea towel until cool, then peel away the skin and chop the flesh.

2 Spray a non-stick frying pan with oil and cook the steak over high heat for 3–4 minutes each side until it is medium–rare. Remove and leave for 5 minutes before cutting into thin slices. Season with a little salt.

3 To make the pesto, finely chop the basil leaves, garlic and pepitas in a food processor. With the motor running, add the oil, orange and lemon juice. Season well.

4 Meanwhile, cook the penne in a large pan of rapidly boiling salted water until al dente. Drain, then toss with the pesto in a large bowl.

5 Add the capsicum pieces, steak slices and mushroom quarters to the penne and toss to distribute evenly. Serve immediately.

NUTRITION PER SERVE Protein 8 g; Fat 5 g; **Carbohydrate 15 g**; Dietary Fibre 2 g; Cholesterol 7 mg; 660 kJ (135 cal)

Cheese and Chive Souffle Tart

80 g (2¾ oz) butter
⅓ cup (40 g/1¼ oz) plain flour
1 cup (250 ml/8 fl oz) cream
⅔ cup (170 g/5½ oz) sour cream
4 eggs, separated
1 cup (130 g/4½ oz) grated Gruyère cheese
3 tablespoons chopped chives

¼ teaspoon ground nutmeg
pinch of cayenne pepper
12 sheets filo pastry

PREPARATION TIME 40 minutes
TOTAL COOKING TIME 55 minutes
SERVES 6–8

1 Preheat the oven to 190°C (375°F/Gas 5). Grease a deep 20 cm (8 inches) loose-based fluted tart tin. Melt half the butter in a pan. Sift in the flour and cook, stirring, for 1 minute. Remove from the heat and gradually whisk in the cream and sour cream.

2 Return to the heat and whisk constantly until the mixture boils and thickens. Remove from the heat and whisk in the egg yolks. Then cover the surface with plastic wrap and set aside to allow to cool slightly. Whisk in the cheese, chives, nutmeg and cayenne.

3 Melt the remaining butter and brush some over each sheet of pastry. Fold each one in half and use to line the tin, allowing the edges to overhang.

4 Beat the egg whites until stiff peaks form, then stir a spoonful into the cheese mixture to loosen it up. Gently fold in the rest of the beaten egg white. Spoon the mixture into the pastry shell and then fold the pastry over the top. Brush the top with the remaining melted butter and bake for 40–45 minutes, or until puffed and golden. Serve immediately.

NUTRITION PER SERVE Protein 10 g; Fat 40 g; **Carbohydrate 15 g**; Dietary Fibre 1 g; Cholesterol 200 mg; 1895 kJ (450 cal)

Pasta and Spinach Timbales

30 g (1 oz) butter
1 tablespoon olive oil
1 onion, chopped
500 g (1 lb) English spinach, cooked
8 eggs, beaten
1 cup (250 ml/8 fl oz) cream
100 g (3½ oz) spaghetti, cooked

½ cup (60 g/2 oz) grated Cheddar
½ cup (60 g/2 oz) grated Parmesan

PREPARATION TIME 15 minutes
TOTAL COOKING TIME 40 minutes
SERVES 6

1 Preheat the oven to moderate 180°C (350°F/Gas 4). Brush six 1-cup (250 ml/8 fl oz) moulds with melted butter or oil. Line the bases with baking paper. Heat the butter and oil together in a frying pan. Add the onion and stir over low heat until tender. Add the well-drained spinach and cook for 1 minute. Remove from the heat and allow to cool. Whisk in the eggs and cream. Stir in the spaghetti, grated cheeses and salt and pepper; stir well. Spoon into the moulds.

2 Place the moulds in a roasting tin. Pour boiling water into the tin to come halfway up the sides of the moulds. Bake for 30–35 minutes or until set. Halfway through cooking, you may need to cover with a sheet of foil to prevent overbrowning. Near the end of cooking time, test the timbales with the point of a knife—the knife should come out clean.

3 Allow the timbales to rest for 15 minutes, then run the point of a knife around the edge of each mould and unmould onto serving plates.

NUTRITION PER SERVE Protein 16 g; Fat 20 g; **Carbohydrate 13 g**; Dietary Fibre 2 g; Cholesterol 260 mg; 1280 kJ (300 cal)

Smoked Salmon Tartlets

250 g (8 oz) cream cheese, softened
1 1/2 tablespoons wholegrain mustard
2 teaspoons Dijon mustard
2 tablespoons lemon juice
2 tablespoons chopped fresh dill
6 sheets puff pastry
300 g (10 oz) smoked salmon, cut into thin strips
65 g (2 1/4 oz) baby capers

PREPARATION TIME 30 minutes + 10 minutes refrigeration
TOTAL COOKING TIME 30 minutes
MAKES 24

1 Preheat the oven to 210°C (415°F/Gas 6–7). Line a large baking tray with baking paper. Mix together the cream cheese, mustards, lemon juice and dill. Cover and refrigerate.

2 Cut four 9 1/2 cm (3 3/4 inch) rounds from each sheet of pastry with a fluted cutter and place on the baking tray. Prick the pastries all over. Cover and refrigerate for 10 minutes.

3 Bake in batches for 7 minutes, remove from the oven and use a spoon to flatten the centre of each pastry. Return to the oven and bake for a further 5 minutes, or until the pastry is golden. Allow to cool, then spread a rounded teaspoon of the cream cheese mixture over each pastry, leaving a 1 cm (1/2 inch) border. Arrange the salmon over the top. Decorate with a few capers.

NUTRITION PER TARTLET Protein 6 g; Fat 15 g; **Carbohydrate 15 g**; Dietary Fibre 0.5 g; Cholesterol 25 mg; 869 kJ (210 cal)

Asian Chicken Noodle Soup

85 g (3 oz) fresh egg noodles
1¼ litres chicken stock
1 tablespoon mirin
2 tablespoons soy sauce
3 cm (1¼ inch) piece fresh ginger, julienned
2 chicken breast fillets, thinly sliced

2 bunches baby bok choy, leaves separated
fresh coriander leaves, to garnish

PREPARATION TIME 10 minutes
TOTAL COOKING TIME 10 minutes
SERVES 4

1 Soak the noodles in boiling water for 1 minute, then drain and set aside. In a large saucepan, heat the stock to simmering, and add the mirin, soy sauce, ginger, chicken and noodles. Cook for 5 minutes, or until the chicken is tender and the noodles are warmed through. Remove any scum from the surface of the soup.

2 Add the bok choy and cook for a further 2 minutes, or until the bok choy leaves have wilted. Serve in deep bowls, garnished with fresh coriander leaves. Serve with sweet chilli sauce, if desired.

Note
Mirin is a sweet rice wine used for cooking. Sweet sherry, with a little sugar added, can be used instead.

NUTRITION PER SERVE Protein 30 g; Fat 3 g; **Carbohydrate 15 g**; Dietary Fibre 1 g; Cholesterol 65 mg; 915 kJ (220 cal)

Minestrone Primavera

¼ cup (60 ml/2 fl oz) olive oil
45 g (1½ oz) pancetta, finely chopped
2 onions, chopped
2 cloves garlic, thinly sliced
2 small celery stalks, sliced
2 litres chicken stock
⅓ cup (50 g/1¾ oz) macaroni
2 zucchini, chopped
2 cups (150 g/5 oz) shredded savoy cabbage
1½ cups (185 g/6 oz) green beans, chopped

1 cup (155 g/5 oz) frozen peas
1 cup (40 g/1¼ oz) shredded English spinach leaves
¼ cup (15 g/½ oz) chopped fresh basil
grated Parmesan, for serving

PREPARATION TIME 15 minutes
TOTAL COOKING TIME 40 minutes
SERVES 4–6

1 Put the oil, pancetta, onion, garlic and celery in a large pan and stir occasionally over low heat for 8 minutes, or until the vegetables are soft but not brown. Add the stock and bring to the boil. Simmer, covered, for 10 minutes.

2 Add the macaroni and boil for 12 minutes, or until almost al dente. Stir in the zucchini, cabbage, beans and peas and simmer for 5 minutes. Add the spinach and basil and simmer for 2 minutes. Season to taste and serve with the grated Parmesan.

NUTRITION PER SERVE Protein 7 g; Fat 20 g; **Carbohydrate 15 g**; Dietary Fibre 6 g; Cholesterol 40 mg; 1030 kJ (250 cal)

Tofu with Carrot and Ginger Sauce

2 x 300 g (10 oz) packets firm tofu
½ cup (125 ml/4 fl oz) freshly squeezed
orange juice
1 tablespoon soft brown sugar
1 tablespoon soy sauce
2 tablespoons chopped fresh coriander leaves
2 cloves garlic, crushed
1 teaspoon grated fresh ginger
2–3 tablespoons oil
1 kg (2 lb) baby bok choy, cut into quarters
lengthways

Carrot and ginger sauce
300 g (10 oz) carrots, chopped
2 teaspoons grated fresh ginger
⅔ cup (170 ml/5½ fl oz) orange juice
½ cup (125 ml/4 fl oz) vegetable stock

PREPARATION TIME 25 minutes + overnight
marinating
TOTAL COOKING TIME 30 minutes
SERVES 6

1 Drain the tofu, then slice each block into six lengthways. Place in a single layer in a flat non-metallic dish. Mix the juice, sugar, soy sauce, coriander, garlic and ginger in a jug, then pour over the tofu. Cover and refrigerate overnight, turning once.

2 Drain the tofu, reserving the marinade. Heat the oil in a large frying pan and cook the tofu in batches over high heat for 2–3 minutes each side, or until golden. Remove and keep warm. Bring the marinade to the boil in a saucepan, then reduce the heat and simmer for 1 minute. Remove from the heat and keep warm.

3 Heat a wok, add the bok choy and 1 tablespoon water and cook, covered, over medium heat for 2–3 minutes, or until tender. Remove and keep warm.

4 Put all the sauce ingredients in a saucepan, bring to the boil, then reduce the heat and simmer, covered, for 5–6 minutes, or until the carrot is tender. Transfer to a food processor and blend until smooth.

5 To serve, divide the bok choy among six plates. Top with some sauce, then the tofu and drizzle on a little of the marinade before serving.

NUTRITION PER SERVE Protein 14 g; Fat 14 g; **Carbohydrate 14 g**; Dietary Fibre 8.5 g; Cholesterol 0 mg; 1034 kJ (246 cal)

Stir-fried Asian Greens and Mushrooms

20 stems Chinese broccoli
4 baby bok choy
100 g (3½ oz) shimeji or enoki mushrooms
100 g (3½ oz) shiitake mushrooms
1 tablespoon soy sauce
2 teaspoons crushed palm sugar
1 tablespoon oil
4 spring onions, cut into short pieces
5 cm (2 inch) fresh ginger, cut into thin strips

1–2 small red chillies, seeded and finely chopped
2–3 cloves garlic, crushed
125 g (4 oz) snow peas, halved
1–2 teaspoons seasoning sauce

PREPARATION TIME 20 minutes
TOTAL COOKING TIME 5 minutes
SERVES 4

1 Remove any tough outer leaves from the Chinese broccoli and bok choy. Cut into 4 cm (1½ inch) pieces across the leaves, including the stems. Wash thoroughly, then drain and dry thoroughly. Wipe the mushrooms with a paper towel and trim the ends. Slice the shiitake mushrooms thickly.

2 Combine the soy sauce and palm sugar with ¼ cup (60 ml/2 fl oz) water. Set aside.

3 Heat the wok until very hot, add the oil and swirl it around to coat the side. Stir-fry the spring onion, ginger, chilli and garlic over low heat for 30 seconds, without browning. Increase the heat to high and add the Chinese broccoli, bok choy and snow peas. Stir-fry for 1–2 minutes, or until the vegetables are wilted.

4 Add the prepared mushrooms and soy sauce mixture. Stir-fry over high heat for 1–2 minutes, or until the mushrooms and sauce are heated through. Sprinkle with the seasoning sauce, to taste, and serve immediately.

NUTRITION PER SERVE Protein 6.5 g; Fat 10 g; **Carbohydrate 15 g**; Dietary Fibre 3 g; Cholesterol 0 mg; 780 kJ (185 cal)

Tortellini with Nutty Herb Sauce

500 g (1 lb) cheese tortellini or ravioli
60 g (2 oz) butter
100 g (3½ oz) walnuts, chopped
100 g (3½ oz) pine nuts
2 tablespoons chopped fresh parsley
2 teaspoons chopped fresh thyme

¼ cup (60 g/2 oz) ricotta cheese
3 tablespoons cream

PREPARATION TIME 15 minutes
TOTAL COOKING TIME 10 minutes
SERVES 4–6

1 Cook the pasta in rapidly boiling water until al dente. Drain and return to the pan.

2 Heat the butter in a heavy-based pan until foaming. Add the walnuts and pine nuts and stir for 5 minutes, or until golden brown. Add the parsley, thyme and salt and pepper.

3 Beat the ricotta with the cream. Toss the sauce and pasta together and top with ricotta cream. Serve immediately.

Variation
Use chopped hazelnuts instead of walnuts.

NUTRITION PER SERVE Protein 12 g; Fat 40 g; **Carbohydrate 13 g**; Dietary Fibre 3 g; Cholesterol 58 mg; 1943 kJ (465 cal)

Yellow Vegetable Curry

¼ cup (60 ml/2 fl oz) oil
1 onion, finely chopped
2 tablespoons yellow curry paste
250 g (8 oz) potato, diced
200 g (6½ oz) zucchini, diced
150 g (5 oz) red capsicum, diced
100 g (3½ oz) beans, trimmed
50 g (1¾ oz) bamboo shoots, sliced

1 cup (250 ml/8 fl oz) vegetable stock
400 ml (13 fl oz) can coconut cream
fresh Thai basil leaves, to garnish

PREPARATION TIME 20 minutes
TOTAL COOKING TIME 45 minutes
SERVES 6

1 Heat the oil in a large saucepan, add the onion and cook over medium heat for 4–5 minutes, or until softened and just turning golden. Add the yellow curry paste and cook, stirring, for 2 minutes, or until fragrant.

2 Add all the vegetables and cook, stirring, over high heat for 2 minutes. Pour in the vegetable stock, reduce the heat to medium and cook, covered, for 15–20 minutes, or until the vegetables are tender. Cook, uncovered, over high heat for 5–10 minutes, or until the sauce has reduced slightly.

3 Stir in the coconut cream, and season with salt. Bring to the boil, stirring frequently, then reduce the heat and simmer for 5 minutes. Garnish with the Thai basil leaves.

NUTRITION PER SERVE Protein 4 g; Fat 24 g; **Carbohydrate 12 g**; Dietary Fibre 3.5 g; Cholesterol 0.5 mg; 1157 kJ (276 cal)

Seafood and Fennel Stew

2 tablespoons olive oil
1 large fennel bulb, thinly sliced
2 leeks, thinly sliced
2 cloves garlic, crushed
1/2 teaspoon paprika
2 tablespoons Pernod or Ricard
200 ml (6 1/2 fl oz) dry white wine
18 mussels, scrubbed and beards removed
1/4 teaspoon saffron threads
1/4 teaspoon thyme leaves

6 baby octopus
16 raw prawns, peeled and deveined
500 g (1 lb) swordfish steaks, cut into large chunks
400 g (13 oz) baby new potatoes
fennel greens, to garnish

PREPARATION TIME 10 minutes
TOTAL COOKING TIME 30 minutes
SERVES 6

1 Heat the oil in a large saucepan over medium heat. Add the fennel, leek and garlic. Stir in the paprika, season lightly and cook for 8 minutes, or until softened. Add the Pernod and wine, and stir for 1 minute, or until reduced by a third.

2 Add the mussels, discarding any open ones. Cover and cook for 1 minute, or until opened, discarding any that do not open. Remove from the pan to cool; remove from the shells and set aside.

3 Add the saffron and thyme to the pan, and cook for 1–2 minutes, stirring. Adjust the seasoning and transfer to a large, flameproof casserole dish.

4 Use a small sharp knife to remove the octopus heads. Grasp the bodies and push the beaks out with your index finger; remove and discard. Slit the heads and remove the gut. Mix the octopus, prawns, fish and potatoes into the stew. Cover and cook gently for 10 minutes, or until tender. Add the mussels, cover and heat through. Garnish with fennel greens and serve.

NUTRITION PER SERVE Protein 65 g; Fat 10 g; **Carbohydrate 15 g**; Dietary Fibre 5 g; Cholesterol 390 mg; 1840 kJ (440 cal)

Chicken and Cashew Stir-fry

oil, for cooking
750 g (1 1/2 lb) chicken thigh fillets, cut into strips
2 egg whites, lightly beaten
1/2 cup (60 g/2 oz) cornflour
2 onions, thinly sliced
1 red capsicum, thinly sliced
200 g (6 1/2 oz) broccoli, cut into bite-sized pieces
2 tablespoons soy sauce

2 tablespoons sherry
1 tablespoon oyster sauce
1/3 cup (50 g/1 3/4 oz) roasted cashews
4 spring onions, diagonally sliced

PREPARATION TIME 30 minutes
TOTAL COOKING TIME 20 minutes
SERVES 4–6

1 Heat the wok until very hot, add 1 tablespoon of the oil and swirl it around to coat the side. Dip about a quarter of the chicken strips into the egg white and then into the cornflour. Add to the wok and stir-fry for 3–5 minutes, or until the chicken is golden brown and just cooked. Drain on paper towels and repeat with the remaining chicken, reheating the wok and adding a little more oil each time.

2 Reheat the wok, add 1 tablespoon of the oil and stir-fry the onion, capsicum and broccoli over medium heat for 4–5 minutes, or until the vegetables have softened slightly. Increase the heat to high and add the soy sauce, sherry and oyster sauce. Toss the vegetables well in the sauce and bring to the boil.

3 Return the chicken to the wok and toss over high heat for 1–2 minutes to heat the chicken and make sure it is entirely cooked through. Season well with salt and freshly cracked pepper. Toss the cashews and spring onion through the chicken mixture, and serve immediately.

Note
When choosing chicken, buy free range if you can as it has a better flavour and texture. Yellowish flesh indicates the chicken has been grain fed but it is not necessarily free range.

NUTRITION PER SERVE Protein 35 g; Fat 15 g; **Carbohydrate 15 g**; Dietary Fibre 3 g; Cholesterol 60 mg; 1375 kJ (330 cal)

Spicy Garlic Chicken

1.4 kg (2 lb 13 oz) chicken pieces
1 small bunch coriander
1 tablespoon olive oil
4 cloves garlic, crushed
2 red onions, thinly sliced
1 large red capsicum, cut into squares
1 teaspoon ground ginger
1 teaspoon chilli powder
1 teaspoon caraway seeds, crushed
1 teaspoon ground turmeric

2 teaspoons ground coriander
2 teaspoons ground cumin
$1/2$ cup (60 g/2 oz) raisins
$1/2$ cup (90 g/3 oz) black olives
1 teaspoon finely grated lemon rind

PREPARATION TIME 30 minutes
TOTAL COOKING TIME 1 hour
SERVES 6

1 Remove any fat and sinew from the chicken (if you prefer, remove the skin as well). Finely chop the bunch of coriander, including the roots.

2 Heat the oil in a large heavy-based pan. Add the garlic, onion, capsicum, ginger, chilli powder, caraway seeds, turmeric, coriander, cumin and coriander roots. Cook over medium heat for 10 minutes.

3 Add the chicken pieces and stir until combined. Add $1\frac{1}{2}$ cups (375 ml/12 fl oz) water and bring to the boil. Reduce the heat and simmer for 45 minutes, or until the chicken is tender and cooked through.

4 Add the raisins, black olives and lemon rind and simmer for a further 5 minutes before serving.

Variation
You can use a whole chicken for this recipe and cut it into 12 pieces yourself.

NUTRITION PER SERVE Protein 33 g; Fat 13 g; **Carbohydrate 13 g**; Dietary Fibre 2 g; Cholesterol 105 mg; 1236 kJ (295 cal)

Penne with Chicken and Mushrooms

30 g (1 oz) butter
1 tablespoon olive oil
1 onion, sliced
1 clove garlic, crushed
60 g (2 oz) prosciutto, chopped
250 g (8 oz) chicken thigh fillets, trimmed and sliced
125 g (4 oz) mushrooms, sliced
1 tomato, peeled, halved and sliced

1 tablespoon tomato paste
1/2 cup (125 ml/4 fl oz) white wine
1 cup (250 ml/8 fl oz) cream
500 g (1 lb) penne
2 tablespoons grated Parmesan, for serving

PREPARATION TIME 15 minutes
TOTAL COOKING TIME 25 minutes
SERVES 4

1 Heat the butter and oil in a large frying pan. Add the onion and garlic and stir over low heat until the onion is tender. Add the prosciutto and fry until crisp.

2 Add the chicken and cook over medium heat for 3 minutes. Add the mushrooms and cook for another 2 minutes. Stir in the tomato and tomato paste and then the wine. Bring to the boil. Reduce the heat and simmer until reduced by half.

3 Stir in the cream, salt and pepper. Bring to the boil. Reduce the heat and simmer until the sauce begins to thicken. Meanwhile, cook the pasta in a large pan of rapidly boiling salted water until al dente. Drain and return to the pan. Add the sauce and toss to combine. Serve immediately, sprinkled with Parmesan.

Hint
If you prefer, you can use chicken mince in this recipe instead of sliced chicken fillets.

NUTRITION PER SERVE Protein 23 g; Fat 60 g; **Carbohydrate 14 g**; Dietary Fibre 3 g; Cholesterol 255 mg; 2888 kJ (700 cal)

Green Chicken Curry

2 cups (500 ml/16 fl oz) coconut cream (do not shake the can—see NOTE)
4 tablespoons green curry paste
2 tablespoons grated palm sugar or soft brown sugar
2 tablespoons fish sauce
4 kaffir lime leaves, finely shredded
1 kg (2 lb) chicken thigh or breast fillets, cut into thick strips

200 g (6½ oz) bamboo shoots, cut into thick strips
100 g (3½ oz) snake beans, cut into 5 cm (2 inch) lengths
½ cup (15 g/½ oz) fresh Thai basil leaves

PREPARATION TIME 40 minutes
TOTAL COOKING TIME 30 minutes
SERVES 4–6

1 Place ½ cup (125 ml/4 fl oz) of the thick coconut cream from the top of the can in a wok, and bring to the boil. Add the curry paste, then reduce the heat and simmer for 15 minutes, or until fragrant and the oil starts to separate from the cream. Add the palm sugar, fish sauce and kaffir lime leaves to the pan.

2 Stir in the remaining coconut cream and the chicken, bamboo shoots and beans, and simmer for 15 minutes, or until the chicken is tender. Stir in the Thai basil and serve with rice.

Note
Do not shake the can of coconut cream because good-quality coconut cream has a layer of very thick cream at the top that has separated from the rest of the cream. This has a higher fat content, which causes it to split or separate more readily than the rest of the coconut cream or milk.

NUTRITION PER SERVE Protein 40 g; Fat 22 g; **Carbohydrate 11 g**; Dietary Fibre 2 g; Cholesterol 85 mg; 1698 kJ (405 cal)

Pork and Lentil Stew

1 tablespoon olive oil
2 onions, chopped
500 g (1 lb) lean diced pork
2 teaspoons sweet Hungarian paprika
1 teaspoon hot paprika
1/2 teaspoon dried thyme
2 tablespoons tomato paste
2 teaspoons soft brown sugar

1/4 cup (60 g/2 oz) red lentils
1 1/2 cups (375 ml/12 fl oz) beef stock
1 tomato
2 tablespoons low-fat plain yoghurt

PREPARATION TIME 20 minutes
TOTAL COOKING TIME 1 hour
SERVES 4

1 Heat the olive oil in a large, deep saucepan over high heat. Add the onion, pork and paprikas, and stir for 3–4 minutes, or until browned.

2 Add the thyme, tomato paste, sugar, lentils, stock, and salt and freshly ground black pepper. Bring to the boil, then reduce the heat to very low and cook, covered, for 20 minutes, stirring occasionally to prevent sticking. Uncover and cook for another 15–20 minutes, or until thickened.

3 Remove from the heat and set aside for 10 minutes. Cut the tomato in half and scoop out the seeds. Slice the flesh into thin strips.

4 Just before serving, stir the yoghurt into the stew. Scatter with the tomato strips and serve with rice, if desired.

NUTRITION PER SERVE Protein 35 g; Fat 8 g; **Carbohydrate 13 g**; Dietary Fibre 4 g; Cholesterol 70 mg; 1110 kJ (265 cal)

Mediterranean Lamb Casserole

1 tablespoon olive oil
750 g (1 1/2 lb) lamb from the bone, diced
1 large onion, sliced
2 cloves garlic, crushed
2 carrots, chopped
2 parsnips, chopped
400 g (13 oz) can chopped tomatoes
2 tablespoons tomato paste

2 teaspoons chopped fresh rosemary
1/2 cup (125 ml/4 fl oz) red wine
1 cup (250 ml/8 fl oz) chicken stock

PREPARATION TIME 15 minutes
TOTAL COOKING TIME 1 hour
SERVES 4

1 Heat the oil in a large saucepan and cook the lamb, in batches, for 3–4 minutes, or until browned. Remove from the pan and keep warm. Add the onion and garlic to the pan and cook for 2–3 minutes, or until the onion is soft.

2 Return the lamb and juices to the pan. Add the carrots, parsnips, tomatoes, tomato paste, rosemary, wine and stock and bring to the boil. Reduce the heat and cover the pan. Simmer the casserole for 50 minutes, or until the lamb is tender and the sauce has thickened.

NUTRITION PER SERVE Protein 45 g; Fat 12 g; **Carbohydrate 12 g**; Dietary Fibre 4.5 g; Cholesterol 125 mg; 1517 kJ (362 cal)

Moussaka

1 kg (2 lb) eggplants
cooking oil spray
400 g (13 oz) lean lamb mince
2 onions, finely chopped
2 cloves garlic, crushed
400 g (13 oz) can tomatoes
1 tablespoon chopped fresh thyme
1 teaspoon chopped fresh oregano
1 tablespoon tomato paste
1/3 cup (80 ml/2¾ fl oz) dry white wine
1 bay leaf
1 teaspoon sugar

Cheese sauce
1¼ cups (315 ml/10 fl oz) skim milk
2 tablespoons plain flour
¼ cup (30 g/1 oz) grated reduced-fat Cheddar
1 cup (250 g/8 oz) ricotta
pinch of cayenne pepper
¼ teaspoon ground nutmeg

PREPARATION TIME 30 minutes
TOTAL COOKING TIME 1 hour 30 minutes
SERVES 6

1 Cut the eggplant into 1 cm (½ inch) thick slices, place in a colander over a large bowl, layering with a generous sprinkling of salt, and leave to stand for 20 minutes. This is to draw out the bitter juices.

2 Lightly spray a non-stick frying pan with oil and brown the lamb mince, in batches if necessary, over medium–high heat. Once all the meat is browned, set aside. Spray the pan again with oil, add the onion and stir continuously for 2 minutes. Add 1 tablespoon water to the pan to prevent sticking. Add the garlic and cook for about 3 minutes, or until the onion is golden brown.

3 Push the undrained tomatoes through a sieve, then discard the contents of the sieve. Return the meat to the pan with the onion. Add the herbs, tomato pulp, tomato paste, wine, bay leaf and sugar. Cover and simmer over low heat for 20 minutes.

4 Preheat a grill. Thoroughly rinse and pat dry the eggplant, place on a grill tray, spray lightly with oil and grill under high heat until golden brown. Turn over, spray lightly with oil and grill until golden brown. Arrange half the eggplant slices over the base of a 1½ litre capacity baking dish. Top with half the meat mixture and then repeat the layers.

5 Preheat the oven to moderate 180°C (350°F/Gas 4). To make the cheese sauce, blend a little of the milk with the flour to form a paste in a small pan. Gradually blend in the remaining milk, stirring constantly over low heat until the milk starts to simmer and thicken. Remove from the heat and stir in the Cheddar, ricotta, cayenne and nutmeg. Pour over the moussaka and bake for 35–40 minutes, or until the cheese is golden brown and the moussaka heated through.

NUTRITION PER SERVE Protein 10 g; Fat 10 g; **Carbohydrate 15 g**; Dietary Fibre 5.5 g; Cholesterol 25 mg; 735 kJ (175 cal)

Chinese Beef in Soy

700 g (1 lb 7 oz) chuck steak, trimmed and cut
into 2 cm (¾ inch) cubes
⅓ cup (80 ml/2¾ fl oz) dark soy sauce
2 tablespoons honey
1 tablespoon wine vinegar
¼ cup (60 ml/2 fl oz) soy bean oil, or oil
4 cloves garlic, chopped
8 spring onions, thinly sliced
1 tablespoon finely grated fresh ginger
2 star anise

½ teaspoon ground cloves
1½ cups (375 ml/12 fl oz) beef stock
½ cup (125 ml/4 fl oz) red wine
sliced spring onions, extra, to garnish

PREPARATION TIME 20 minutes + overnight
marinating
TOTAL COOKING TIME 1 hour 45 minutes
SERVES 4

1 Place the meat in a non-metallic dish. Combine
the soy sauce, honey and vinegar in a small bowl,
then pour over the meat. Cover with plastic wrap
and marinate for at least 2 hours, or preferably
overnight. Drain, reserving the marinade, and pat
the cubes dry.

2 Place 1 tablespoon of the oil in a saucepan and
brown the meat in 3 batches, for 3–4 minutes per
batch—add another tablespoon of oil, if necessary.
Remove the meat. Add the remaining oil and fry
the garlic, spring onion, ginger, star anise and
cloves for 1–2 minutes, or until fragrant.

3 Return all the meat to the pan, and add the
reserved marinade, stock and wine. Bring to the
boil, then reduce the heat and simmer, covered,
for 1¼ hours. Cook, uncovered, for a further
15 minutes, or until the sauce is syrupy and the
meat is tender.

4 Garnish with the extra sliced spring onion and
serve immediately.

NUTRITION PER SERVE Protein 37 g; Fat 20 g; **Carbohydrate 12 g**; Dietary Fibre 0.5 g; Cholesterol 117 mg; 1657 kJ (395 cal)

Steak with Roasted Red Onion Sauce

250 g (8 oz) red onions, thinly sliced
500 g (1 lb) pickling onions
2 cloves garlic
1 tablespoon olive oil
750 g (1 1/2 lb) Roma tomatoes
1/2 teaspoon salt
2 tablespoons chopped fresh oregano
220g (7 oz) can Italian peeled tomatoes

2 teaspoons muscatel liqueur or brandy
2 teaspoons soft brown sugar
4 scotch or rump fillet steaks, trimmed

PREPARATION TIME 20 minutes
TOTAL COOKING TIME 1 hour 20 minutes
SERVES 4

1 Preheat the oven to moderately hot 200°C (400°F/Gas 6). Place the red onion, pickling onions and garlic cloves in a large roasting tin with half the olive oil. Roll the onions in the oil so that they are lightly coated.

2 Halve the tomatoes lengthways and add to the tin. Drizzle with the remaining olive oil, salt and oregano and roast for 1 hour.

3 Use a pair of kitchen scissors to roughly cut up the canned tomatoes, while they are still in the tin. Spoon the chopped tomatoes and their juice into the roasting tin, taking care not to break up the roasted tomatoes. Drizzle the muscatel or brandy over the top and sprinkle with the brown sugar. Return to the oven and roast for a further 20 minutes.

4 Chargrill the steaks on a lightly oiled chargrill pan until cooked to your liking. Serve with the hot sauce.

Serving suggestion
This sauce is a great low-fat condiment for serving with grilled meats at barbecues.

NUTRITION PER SERVE Protein 60 g; Fat 15 g; **Carbohydrate 13 g**; Dietary Fibre 5 g; Cholesterol 143 mg; 1900 kJ (450 cal)
NOTE Potato shown as a serving suggestion. Carbohydrate content not included in nutrition per serve.

Steak and Kidney Stew

1 kg (2 lb) chuck steak, trimmed
8 lamb's kidneys
1/4 cup (60 ml/2 fl oz) oil
1 rasher bacon, rind removed, cut into long, thin strips
40 g (1 1/4 oz) butter
1 large onion, chopped
300 g (10 oz) button mushrooms, halved
1 cup (250 ml/8 fl oz) Muscat
2–3 cloves garlic, crushed
1/4 teaspoon ground allspice

1/2 teaspoon paprika
2 teaspoons coriander seeds, lightly crushed
1 tablespoon wholegrain mustard
1 cup (250 ml/8 fl oz) beef stock
2–3 tablespoons soft brown sugar
1–2 teaspoons fresh thyme
1–2 teaspoons fresh rosemary

PREPARATION TIME 35 minutes
TOTAL COOKING TIME 2 hours 30 minutes
SERVES 4–6

1 Cut the steak into 2–3 cm (1 inch) cubes. Cut the kidneys in half, remove the core and any fat, then slice them in half again.

2 Heat 1 teaspoon of the oil in a large, heavy-based saucepan. Add the bacon and cook over medium heat until just crisp. Remove and set aside.

3 Heat 2 tablespoons of the oil and 30 g (1 oz) of the butter in the pan. Brown the steak cubes in batches, then set aside.

4 Add the onion to the pan and cook for 3 minutes, or until soft and golden. Add the mushrooms and cook, stirring, for 3 minutes, until starting to brown. Stir in half the Muscat and simmer for 3–4 minutes. Remove and set aside.

5 Add the remaining oil and butter to the pan. Stir in the garlic, allspice, paprika and coriander, and cook for 1 minute. Add the kidney and cook until just starting to brown. Stir in the mustard and remaining Muscat, and simmer for 2 minutes.

6 Stir in the bacon, steak, onion and mushrooms. Stir in the stock, bring to the boil, then reduce the heat, cover and simmer for 1 hour. Add the sugar. Simmer, covered, for 40 minutes, then uncovered for 20 minutes, stirring in the herbs during the last 10 minutes.

NUTRITION PER SERVE Protein 40 g; Fat 20 g; **Carbohydrate 15 g**; Dietary Fibre 2 g; Cholesterol 155 mg; 1830 kJ (440 cal)
NOTE Potato shown as a serving suggestion. Carbohydrate content not included in nutrition per serve.

Spiced Pears

1/3 cup (80 ml/2¾ fl oz) kecap manis
3 tablespoons soy sauce
2 teaspoons sesame oil
1 teaspoon five-spice powder
6 ripe beurre bosc pears, unpeeled and quartered

PREPARATION TIME 10 minutes
TOTAL COOKING TIME 1 hour
SERVES 8

1 Preheat the oven to slow 150°C (300°F/Gas 2). Line two shallow baking trays with foil and place a wire rack in each tray. In a large bowl, mix the kecap manis, soy sauce, sesame oil and five-spice powder.

2 Brush the quartered pears all over with the soy mixture. Place apart, skin-side-down, in a single layer on the racks. Bake for 30 minutes. Brush the pears again with the marinade and continue baking for a further 30 minutes, or until the pears are tender and caramelised around the edge.

3 Serve the pears warm or at room temperature with cheese and biscuits or as an accompaniment to cold meat.

Hint
The foil will catch any excess drops of the soy mixture. If the mixture scorches or burns during the cooking process, replace the foil lining halfway through the cooking time.

Note
Kecap manis (ketjap manis) is an Indonesian sauce similar to—but sweeter than—soy sauce. It is generally flavoured with garlic and star anise.

It is important that you use ripe pears for best results in this recipe.

Serving suggestion
These roasted pears go very well with roast duck, pork, chicken, quail or an assortment of smoked meats.

NUTRITION PER SERVE Protein 1 g; Fat 1 g; **Carbohydrate 15 g**; Dietary Fibre 2.5 g; Cholesterol 0 mg; 280 kJ (65 cal)

Lemon Berry Cheesecake

60 g (2 oz) plain sweet biscuits, finely crushed
30 g (1 oz) butter, melted
300 g (10 oz) ricotta
2 tablespoons caster sugar
2 x 130 g (4 oz) tubs low-fat French vanilla fromage frais
2 x 130 g (4 oz) tubs low-fat Lemon Tang fromage frais
2 teaspoons finely grated lemon rind
2 tablespoons lemon juice

1 tablespoon gelatine
2 egg whites
250 g (8 oz) strawberries, halved

PREPARATION TIME 25 minutes + overnight refrigeration
SERVES 12

1 Lightly oil and line the base and side of a 20 cm (8 inch) springform tin with plastic wrap. Combine the biscuits and butter in a bowl and press evenly over the base of the tin. Refrigerate while making the filling.

2 Combine the ricotta and sugar in a food processor until smooth. Add all the fromage frais, the lemon rind and juice, then mix well.

3 Put ¼ cup (60 ml/2 fl oz) water in a small bowl, sprinkle the gelatine in an even layer onto the surface and leave to go spongy. Bring a small pan of water to the boil, remove from the heat and put the gelatine bowl in the pan. The water should come halfway up the side of the bowl. Stir the gelatine until clear and dissolved, then cool slightly.

4 Stir the gelatine mixture into the ricotta mixture, then transfer to a large bowl.

5 Beat the egg whites until soft peaks form, then gently fold into the ricotta mixture. Pour the mixture into the tin and refrigerate for several hours or overnight, until set. Carefully remove from the tin by removing the side of the pan and gently easing the plastic from underneath. Decorate with the halved strawberries.

NUTRITION PER SERVE Protein 8.5 g; Fat 6 g; **Carbohydrate 12 g**; Dietary Fibre 1 g; Cholesterol 21.5 mg; 560 kJ (140 Cal)

Macadamia and White Chocolate Cookies

1 1/3 cups (180 g/6 oz) macadamia nuts
1 egg
3/4 cup (140 g/4 1/2 oz) soft brown sugar
2 tablespoons white sugar
1 teaspoon vanilla essence
1/2 cup (125 ml/4 fl oz) oil
1/2 cup (60 g/2 oz) plain flour
1/4 cup (30 g/1 oz) self-raising flour

1/4 teaspoon cinnamon
1/2 cup (30 g/1 oz) shredded coconut
3/4 cup (130 g/4 1/2 oz) white chocolate bits

PREPARATION TIME 15 minutes + 30 minutes refrigeration
TOTAL COOKING TIME 20 minutes
MAKES about 25

1 Put the nuts on a baking tray and bake for 5 minutes, or until lightly toasted. Cool and roughly chop.

2 Using electric beaters, beat the egg and sugars in a bowl until light and fluffy. Add the vanilla and oil. Using a wooden spoon, stir in the sifted flours, cinnamon, coconut, macadamias and chocolate, and mix well. Refrigerate for 30 minutes. Preheat the oven to moderate 180°C (350°F/Gas 4). Grease and line two baking trays.

3 Form rounded tablespoons of the mixture into balls and place on the baking trays, pressing the mixture together with your fingertips if crumbly. Bake for 12–15 minutes, or until golden. Cool slightly on the trays, then transfer to a wire rack.

Variation
Dark chocolate bits can be used instead of white chocolate.

NUTRITION PER COOKIE Protein 1.5 g; Fat 10 g; **Carbohydrate 13 g**; Dietary Fibre 0.5 g; Cholesterol 8 mg; 695 kJ (165 cal)

Chocolate-almond Tarts

1 cup (125 g/4 oz) plain flour
60 g (2 oz) unsalted butter, chilled and cubed
1 tablespoon icing sugar
1 tablespoon lemon juice

Filling
1 egg
$1/3$ cup (90 g/3 oz) caster sugar
2 tablespoons cocoa powder

$1/2$ cup (90 g/3 oz) ground almonds
3 tablespoons cream
3 tablespoons apricot jam
18 blanched almonds

PREPARATION TIME 40 minutes
TOTAL COOKING TIME 15 minutes
MAKES 18 tarts

1   Preheat the oven to 180°C (350°F/Gas 4). Lightly grease two 12-cup shallow patty tins. Mix the flour, butter and icing sugar in a food processor for 10 seconds, or until fine and crumbly. Add the juice and process until the dough forms a ball. Roll out between two sheets of baking paper to 6 mm ($1/4$ inch) thick. Cut rounds with a 7 cm ($2^3/4$ inch) fluted cutter to line the tins and refrigerate for 20 minutes.

2   Beat the egg and sugar with electric beaters until thick and pale. Sift the cocoa over the top. With a flat-bladed knife, stir in the ground almonds and cream.

3   Place a dab of jam in the centre of each pastry base. Spoon the filling into the bases and place an almond in the centre of each one. Bake for 15 minutes, or until puffed and set on top. Leave in the tins for 5 minutes, then cool on wire racks.

NUTRITION PER TART Protein 2 g; Fat 8 g; **Carbohydrate 15 g**; Dietary Fibre 1 g; Cholesterol 23 mg; 560 kJ (135 cal)

Index